"Johnson and Reynolds are provocateurs in the best sense of that word, and *Against All Gods* is sure to arouse considerable debate and reflection. This is not another apologetic response to the new atheists. It is a cultural analysis and critique of their claims. It reads like a detective novel and conveys powerful, important ideas to the reader. I couldn't put it down."

J. P. Moreland, Distinguished Professor of Philosophy, Biola University, and author of *The God Question*

"This superb work by Phillip E. Johnson and John Mark Reynolds is both an informed response to the new atheism and simultaneously an invitation for ongoing conversation with those who question the truth claims of the Christian faith. I have longed to have a volume like this one to share with my colleagues in the world of higher education. *Against All Gods* is timely, convincing, readable and accessible; it is a privilege to recommend this little book to a wide audience, with the hope that it will find its way into the hands of university students across the land."

David S. Dockery, President, Union University

"Rather than engaging in specific critiques of the new atheism, Phil Johnson and John Mark Reynolds add their voices to the increasing scholarly chorus that decries the real oppressor in these and related discussions: unexamined naturalistic presuppositions that reject alternative ideas without a hearing. Declaring that uncritical attitudes and a lack of appreciation for ancient writings lie behind many recent criticisms of Christianity, the authors call for open discussion of the relevant issues. This volume is a treat to read, featuring a succinct, straightforward and easily digestible text that successfully treats issue after issue."

Gary R. Habermas, Distinguished Research Professor, Liberty University and Theological Seminary

AGAINST ALL GODS

WHAT'S RIGHT AND WRONG ABOUT THE NEW ATHEISM

Phillip E. Johnson
& John Mark Reynolds

IVP Books

An imprint of InterVarsity Press
Downers Grove, Illinois

InterVarsity Press
P.O. Box 1400, Downers Grove, IL 60515-1426
World Wide Web: www.ivpress.com
E-mail: email@ivpress.com

InterVarsity Press® is the book-publishing division of InterVarsity Christian Fellowship/USA®,
a movement of students and faculty active on campus at hundreds of universities, colleges and
schools of nursing in the United States of America, and a member movement of the International
Fellowship of Evangelical Students. For information about local and regional activities, write
Public Relations Dept., InterVarsity Christian Fellowship/USA, 6400 Schroeder Rd., P.O. Box
7895, Madison, WI 53707-7895, or visit the IVCF website at <www.intervarsity.org>.

All Scripture quotations, unless otherwise indicated, are taken from the New American
Standard Bible®, copyright 1960, 1962, 1963, 1968, 1971, 1972, 1973, 1975, 1977, 1995 by
The Lockman Foundation. Used by permission.

Design: Cindy Kiple
Images: Grant Faint/Getty Images

ISBN 978-0-8308-3738-0

Printed in the United States of America ∞

Library of Congress Cataloging-in-Publication Data

Johnson, Phillip E., 1940-
    Against all gods: what's right and wrong about the new atheism/
Phillip E. Johnson and John Mark Reynolds.
        p. cm.
    Includes bibliographical references and index.
    ISBN 978-0-8308-3738-0 (pbk.: alk. paper)
    1. Apologetics   2. Christianity and atheism.   3. Religion and
science.   I. Reynolds, John Mark, 1963-   II. Title.
    BT1212.J65 2010
    261.2'1—dc22

                                                        2010000182

P   21   20   19   18   17   16   15   14   13   12   11   10   9   8   7   6   5   4   3   2   1

Y   27   26   25   24   23   22   21   20   19   18   17   16   15   14   13   12   11   10

CONTENTS

INTRODUCTION

Phillip E. Johnson

After a second stroke in December of 2004, I was not in the mood to write another book. Writing a book takes not only time but energy and commitment, and I couldn't for a while think of a subject that interested me enough to get started. It was only when I read in 2006 of the spectacular growth in the sales of books advocating atheism that I found a topic I really wanted to write about.

The group of writers that interested me is called "The New Atheists," but it is not their arguments that are new. They argue, as atheists long have, that science leaves no room for the supernatural and that religion leads to conflict which could be avoided if religion were abolished. What is new about these writers is that they are "evangelical" atheists. They are determined to convert the whole society to atheism, and they think they can do it, however impossible that may seem at present.

They intend to copy the success which gay activists have

had in the United States, nearly convincing the judges and intellectuals that same-sex relationships are as normal as man-woman relationships and should be treated similarly for legal purposes, no matter what the public thinks about the subject. They consider their own arguments so convincing that eventually everyone will be too embarrassed to disagree.

I saw the tremendous surge of book sales by atheist authors not as a matter to lament but as a challenge that might make university life more interesting than it has been, and would force Christians to clarify their thinking. My decision to start the book was made easier when I was able to enlist my friend John Mark Reynolds in being a coauthor. John has enormous energy and a solid grounding in subjects in which my own education has not been thorough. Our attitude toward the surge in atheism is that it opens up an opportunity for university discussions in and out of the classroom that can make teaching more exciting for the instructor and for the students. With that in mind, our intention is not to attack the atheists but to explore the case they are making, in the hope of encouraging classroom instructors to put the arguments for atheism on the table for academic consideration.

What I like about atheists is that although they tend to give the wrong answers, they also tend to raise the right questions. The implicit message of the university curriculum for some decades now has been that God has not been a subject worth thinking about. The new atheists we are writing about in this book want to talk a lot about God because they think that belief in God is a very bad thing and that religion with any supernatural element should no longer be tolerated as benign, even if misguided. It is better to be regarded as a menace rather than as a nonentity, and so

I think that the new atheist books are likely to have a healthy effect on the position of religion within the university. The resulting tumult legitimates critical discussion of questions that have been swept under the rug for decades by the intellectual classes.

At the same time that the professors have been ignoring the subject of religion as not worth their attention, students have been showing an increased interest in the subject in their private lives. I saw the chaplain of Harvard University quoted in a newspaper story recently as saying that there are more evangelical Christians at Harvard today than at any time since the seventeenth century. There is thus a radical disconnect between what the students are thinking and what the professors have been willing to discuss. Our position in this book is that the arguments for atheism should be taken seriously and considered both respectfully and critically. One of the healthy aspects of the current atheist movement is that the atheists who are selling so many books say that they want everything to be put on the table for criticism, with nothing held back as too sensitive for such examination. They say that they deplore the fact that in some circles it is considered unacceptable to criticize a religion because somebody might be offended. We agree that religion, like any other topic, should be subject to careful, critical and fair-minded examination. I think that the atheists do not realize how certain topics within their own philosophy have been held off the table and protected from criticism. They use the grounds that it is an unacceptable insult to the science community to challenge the naturalistic worldview that has become associated with science.

We are very much in an agreement with our atheist

friends that everybody's views should be subject to analysis and criticism, and nobody should be able to say this is something you simply must accept because certain powerful opinion makers in our society demand that you leave it alone. We will make certain critical points about what the atheists are writing. However, our desire is not to shut down the discussion with a resounding rebuttal but rather to encourage careful examination of the issues both inside the university classroom and outside. We believe that the truth can only benefit from the uninhibited discussion of the issues that divide people. For this reason we welcome the surge that the new atheism represents; it is interesting and we will all profit from discussing the issues that the atheists are raising, if we are also careful to maintain a critical stance toward dogmatic claims that have not been justified by the evidence or by logic.

John Mark Reynolds and I wrote our chapters separately and then revised them jointly to produce a single coherent book, which expresses both of our views. I (Johnson) wrote the introduction, the epilogue and the first five chapters. Reynolds wrote chapters six through eight and did the final editing of the manuscript.

1

INTRODUCING THE NEW ATHEISTS

Phillip E. Johnson

In 2006 and 2007, newspapers and magazines in America began taking notice of an extraordinary phenomenon. Although polling data and election results seemed to confirm that the people of the United States are overwhelmingly Christians in a traditional sense, books by a new breed of aggressive scientific atheists were recording astonishingly high sales, suggesting that even the Bible believers are attracted by a vigorous advocacy of atheism.

Up to the present time, scientific authorities have thought that the only way to persuade the American public to accept the Darwinian theory of evolution is to reassure them that a fully naturalistic account of the history of life poses no threat to a religious belief in the existence of God. Only fundamentalist varieties of religion that ought to be discarded anyway are threatened by evolutionary science, these authorities say.

The new breed of scientific atheists dismisses these reassurances as dishonest, reflecting a cowardly spirit of appeasement. Instead of appeasing the forces of unreason, why not go to the root of the problem and show that the very concept of a supernatural being or force is delusional, and leads only to harm. These atheists are exhilarated by the unbroken record of success they think science has achieved in explaining the world without allowing room for God, and by their own success in selling books and gathering publicity.

Ebullient in one way, they are maddened by the influence of conservative Christians in American public affairs and by the persistence of public skepticism toward the Darwinian theory and its worldview. Worried by this widespread skepticism and its recent spread from America to the once securely post-Christian nations of Europe, they have decided to go on the attack to demolish what Dawkins calls "the God delusion" before it can do still more damage to their program of persuading the world to embrace a scientific rationalism based on the assumption that nature is all that exists, and therefore that God is a illusion that rationality must discard. To that end, they are entering the public arena with the gloves off, determined to complete the demolition of theism by aggressively pressing their claim that belief in a supernatural creator is both absurd and evil, even if this bold stance offends evolution-friendly liberal Christians.

ASKING THE RIGHT QUESTIONS

Americans know that some trend or conflict is really big news when they see it on the cover of *Time* magazine. *Time*'s cover story for the November 13, 2006, issue was titled "Science vs. God." It featured a spirited debate over God's existence between the vehemently atheist biologist Richard

Dawkins and the Christian geneticist Francis Collins, director of the U.S. government's successful project to sequence the human genome.

The debate interested me less for what the debaters said than for the way the magazine's editors framed the subject, and why they thought it worthy of a *Time* cover in late 2006. Since Dawkins says that science and religion (defined as belief in God) are antithetical, and Collins says they are not, for *Time* to define the subject as "God versus science" was to cast Dawkins in the role of science pursuing a retreating deity. A debate billed as "Dawkins vs. God" would have given God a much less formidable opponent, and so might have made the cover less likely to attract attention.

I suspect that most of the scientists who saw the magazine winced at the prospect that Richard Dawkins speaks for science, but that doesn't necessarily imply that they will demand that *Time* correct the misunderstanding, so much of the public may go on assuming that Dawkins actually does speak for science because of what they read on the cover of *Time*.

Time's writer David Van Biema introduced the debate by explaining that the live issue today is not whether Darwinian evolution can withstand the criticisms of creationists but whether religion (defined for this occasion as belief in God) can survive the progress of science. Today, wrote Van Biema, "the anti-religion position is being promoted with increasing insistence by scientists angered by the intelligent design movement and 'excited, perhaps intoxicated, by their disciplines' increasing ability to map, quantify and change the nature of human experience."

When the debate proper started, Dawkins stated that Darwin's theory of evolution by natural selection does much more than simply contradict the Genesis story. In addition to that, it refutes the strongest argument from the physical world for the existence of God: the argument from design. This argument, in Dawkins's words, is that "living things are so beautiful and elegant and so apparently purposeful, they could only have been made by an intelligent designer." Dawkins thinks that Darwin forever discredited the argument from design by proving that the appearance of design is actually due to

> gradual, incremental natural improvements starting from very simple beginnings and working up step by tiny incremental step to more complexity, more elegance, and more adaptive perfection. Each step is not too improbable for us to countenance, but when you add them up cumulatively over millions of years, you get these monsters of improbability, like the human brain and the rain forest.

Darwin's success "should warn us against ever assuming that because something is complicated, God must have done it."

But is Darwin's success really so all-encompassing? The human brain and the rain forest certainly exist, but that either was created by an accumulation of random errors in copying DNA might be doubted, if the claim were thought to require experimental verification rather than merely the support of a consensus of biologists today. (See chapter four on "The Darwinian Worldview" for more on this subject.)

Collins did not dispute Dawkins on Darwin's success, but raised the possibility that God could have activated evolution, not controlling it, but foreseeing that it would turn out as he wished. Dawkins shot back that this explanation is implausible: "If God wanted to create humans, it would be slightly odd that he should choose the extraordinarily round-about way of waiting for 10 billion years before life got started and then waiting for another 4 billion years until you got human beings capable of worshipping and sinning and all the other things religious people are interested in."

Collins interjected that, if God did not wish to make his existence obvious to us, then it would "have been sensible for him to use the mechanism of evolution without posting obvious road signs to reveal his role in creation."

If Dawkins were ever to become a Christian, he would surely be a young-earth creationist. The possibility is admittedly remote, but perhaps such a Damascus Road turnabout is not entirely out of the question. Because Dawkins has over the last several decades been drawn so obsessively to denouncing belief in God, despite the urging of his scientific peers to remain aloof from the subject as they do, some readers of Dawkins think they see signs that something about God troubles his spirit. One thing we know is that Dawkins is not overreacting, as some have imagined, to an unpleasant childhood experience with an adult who tried to bully him to conform to conventional religion, because he very convincingly denies ever having had such an experience. (To confirm this denial, read page 11 of *The God Delusion*.) That leaves me to wonder just what *has* produced an anger of toward God that seems too passionate to proceed from intellectual considerations alone.

Following their brief exchange over evolution, the *Time* debate turned to the origin of the universe. Collins employed what cosmologists call the "fine-tuning" argument. Dawkins did not dispute Collins's suggestion that, if the six or more basic physical characteristics of our universe had varied even slightly, life would not exist. Collins reasoned from this premise that "if you are willing to consider the possibility of a designer, this [that a designer fine tuned the universe for life] becomes a rather plausible explanation."

Dawkins replied that Darwin showed us that a natural explanation is always available for a complex natural phenomenon, even where we find one hard to imagine. More specifically, Dawkins added that the cosmic fine-tuning can already be explained by the multiverse hypothesis. This posits that ours is only one of a huge number of alternate universes. With so many universes, it is not unlikely that one would just happen to have the precise conditions needed for the evolution of intelligent, civilized life forms. Collins responded that "the simpler explanation is the existence of God rather than the multiverse hypothesis," which, he objected, "seems quite a stretch of the imagination." Dawkins retorted that "What I can't understand is why you invoke improbability and yet you will not admit that you are shooting yourself in the foot by postulating something just as improbable."

The debate was thus reduced to the question of whether God's existence is more or less improbable than the existence of a great many alternate (and unobservable) universes. Science has presented us with that question, but no observation or experiment can ever answer it for us. Once scientists start comparing the probability of alternate universes with that of God's existence, they have left the discipline of empirical science far behind and launched themselves into a realm of philosophical speculation, where everyone can believe as he or she likes, because no scientific test can determine who is right.

Dawkins has told me that he loathes lawyers, but he has some of the personal traits of a trial lawyer himself, especially the aggressiveness. Collins is a more reflective, mild-mannered person, so, in a sense, he was overmatched even if *Time* had assigned him to debate only Dawkins, rather than "science." Despite that handicap, a jury might have found Collins more persuasive than Dawkins, because Dawkins, who relies heavily upon ex cathedra pronouncements and intimidation, tends to come across as a bully rather than an embodiment of scientific reason.

THE NOVEMBER COVER ARTICLE IN *WIRED*

Wired is a magazine for technophiles, typically crammed with articles and advertisements touting the latest in electronic gadgetry. The November 2006 issue, however, was mostly devoted to a long and provocative article by Gary Wolf about the resurgent scientific atheism described by *Time* in its introduction to the Dawkins-Collins debate. Some scientists, no longer content to defend their territory from outside interference, have decided that belief in God is an evil no longer to be tolerated. Much of their indignation is directed at acts of Islamic terrorism, but they cast the blame broadly at "religion," and thus condemn Christians as similarly misguided.

The target of this verbal jihad is not so much religious fundamentalists as liberal or moderate Christians, whom they accuse of providing respectable cover for the fundamentalists, or even lukewarm agnostics like Gary Wolf, who shirk their duty to engage in the battle on the side of atheism. These latter are firmly told that neutrality in the war against God is not an option. As Wolf puts it,

We are called out, we fence sitters, and told to help exorcise this debilitating curse: the curse of faith. The New Atheists will not let us off the hook simply because we are not doctrinaire believers. They condemn not just belief in God but respect for belief in God. Religion is not only wrong; it's evil.

Now that the battle has been joined, there's no excuse for shirking. Three writers have sounded this call to arms. They are Richard Dawkins, Sam Harris and Daniel Dennett. Gary Wolf set out to interview all three for his *Wired* article. He wanted to find out "what it would mean to enlist in the war against faith."

One thing it would mean, Wolf learned, is revising some of our views about human rights and family relationships. Dawkins says he is willing to allow adults to believe whatever they like, but not to teach their religious beliefs to their children, because to him such beliefs consist of "manifest falsehoods," and to inflict them on children is a form of child abuse.

Although I disagree with Dawkins about as much as anyone could, there are some things about the man I can't help liking. One of those things is his irrepressible habit of saying what he thinks to be the truth, even though he knows that his in-your-face atheism horrifies his more prudent allies, who believe that the only way to overcome public opposition to a materialist theory of evolution is to deny or disguise its negative implications for religion. Dawkins says what he really believes, not minding if the bald truth horrifies the lawyers and spin doctors on his own team.

Another thing I like is that Dawkins has a talent for directing attention to the right questions, even when he insists on the wrong answer. For example, he is one of those atheists who can't stop talking about God, and so he continually reminds his listeners of how important is to find out whether God exists. This is both more honest and more perceptive than pretending that God's existence is unnecessary to discuss because it doesn't much matter anyway. By insisting so vehemently that God does not exist, Dawkins implicitly invites others to argue to the contrary. He may even inspire educational institutions to design courses comparing the relative merits of theism and scientific materialism as worldviews. This may be why more pragmatic materialists urge him to drop the subject.

Gary Wolf considered joining the new atheist crusade, but in the end he backed away because he concluded that the new atheist movement cannot achieve its objectives. "People see a contradiction in its tone of certainty." Contemptuous of the faith of others, its proponents never doubt their own belief. They are fundamentalists. "I hear this protest dozens of times," Wolf wrote. "It comes up in every conversation. Even those who might side with the new atheists are repelled by their strident tone." One way to interpret the new wave of scientific atheism is that it is a regression to the time, a few centuries ago, when most people assumed that there could be no peace in a realm unless the people and the ruler all shared the same religion. Since then we have grown accustomed to religious pluralism and have learned that people of differing religions can live peacefully together in the same nation if they approach their disagreements in a spirit of mutual respect. The generally harmonious relations of Protestants, Catholics, Mormons and Jews in twentieth-century America provides a powerful example. Perhaps Dawkins and Harris want to return to the principle that there can be only one religion in a nation, and it must be their own religion. I wonder if proceeding on this basis is a recipe for unending civil conflict.

Despite poll figures that show that only a tiny fraction of Americans are atheists, Richard Dawkins and Sam Harris are optimistic about their chances for eventual political success. Dawkins estimates that there are a great many silent atheists in America, whose existence is overlooked by public opinion polls, but who will join the atheist campaign when enough others have taken a public stand. Dawkins thinks that atheists today are in much the same position as gays were in a generation ago, before gay liberation movements rallied public and judicial support. Harris likes to muse about how public opinion has been turned around in the past on other issues, such as slavery. "At some point," Harris writes, "clinging to a belief in God will become too embarrassing to continue. At that point, atheism will be the dominant religious position in America and the world." Yes, if we ever reach that point.

I found the *Wired* article informative and provocative, but it described only three authors: the philosopher Daniel Dennett, the neuroscience graduate student Sam Harris, and Richard Dawkins, plus a few supporters, so I could not tell whether the "new wave of atheism" encompassed more than a few extremists, however many of their books a curious public is buying. I am among those buyers, after all, and not because I am attracted to atheism. I wasn't sure anything worth further notice was going on until I read an article in the November 21, 2006, *New York Times* by George Johnson titled "A Free-for-All on Science and Religion."

THE UPROAR AT THE SALK INSTITUTE

Johnson's article reported on a science and religion forum held at the Salk Institute for Biological Studies in La Jolla,

California. The article reported that this conference veered from the usual polite banalities that the subject tends to evoke and began to resemble the founding convention of a political party built on a single plank: "In a world dangerously charged with ideology, science needs to take on an evangelistic role, vying with religion as a teller of the greatest story ever told." Planetarium director Neil deGrasse Tyson lamented that too many scientists, even including some members of the elite National Academy, still believe in a God who answers prayer. Astronomer Carolyn Porco said,

> We should let the success of the religious formula guide us. Let's teach our children from a young age about the story of the universe and its incredible richness and beauty. It is already so much more glorious and awesome—and even comforting—than anything offered by any scripture or god concept I know.

To illustrate her point, Dr. Porco displayed a picture taken by the Cassini spacecraft of Saturn and its glowing rings eclipsing the Sun, revealing in the shadow a barely noticeable speck called Earth.

The "free-for-all" story convinced me that there are considerably more people in the scientific community angry enough to launch an anti-God crusade than just the three authors described in the *Wired* article by Gary Wolf. Still, the lust for battle is far from unanimous. Some heated dissenting comments at the forum showed that any anti-God offensive will draw opposition from scientists who, whether they believe in God or not, think that science should not get into an open fight with religion, and that the program of converting the world to scientific atheism rests on a thoroughly unscientific disregard of reality. Still the debate was only over how to engage in conflict, not whether the conflict exists. The determination to take the offensive seems to be born more of desperation than triumphalism.

According to the *New York Times* article, "With a rough consensus that the grand stories of evolution by natural selection and the blossoming of the universe from the Big Bang are losing out in the intellectual marketplace, most of the discussion came down to strategy. How can science fight back without appearing to be just one more ideology?"

From all this information, I concluded that the new atheist crusaders pose a greater problem for the ruling scientific authorities, the men and women I call the mandarins of science, than for the Christians whom their campaign is meant to discredit. Although the new wave of atheists like to imagine that religion has hitherto been exempt from frank criticism, Christians are in fact quite accustomed to it, and probably need it to help us avoid complacency.

The problem for the mandarins is that the new wave of atheists may gain enough of a following in science to pressure the reigning institutional authorities to take a stand for or against their claim that the logic of Darwinism supports atheism. The mandarins of science cannot endorse the atheist campaign, however, without making it appear that they have been lying to the public for decades by their constant assurances that science and nonfundamentalist religion are compatible. I have little doubt that a substantial number of the mandarins agree with Dawkins in private, but do not want to say so openly for fear of encouraging still more public skepticism. The problem will become acute if the new wave of atheists can recruit enough support among scientists that the mandarins cannot disavow the movement without facing a revolt in their own camp.

What needs to happen in these circumstances is that all the contested issues regarding the relationship between science and atheism ought to be analyzed fairly and thoroughly by our universities, both in conferences of scholars and with students in classrooms. Does the logic of a naturalistic science support atheism? If not, why are so many scientists convinced that it does? Dawkins and his allies may be wrong, but surely their reasons for taking such a bold position deserve serious examination. Our hopes of coming to the truth about whether Darwinian science and theistic religion are incompatible can only be satisfied if there is genuine intellectual confrontation between competing viewpoints in the universities, where all the most sensitive issues can be brought out into the open without some federal judge breaking in to rule that only one position may be considered.

FINDING THE TRUE OPPRESSOR

Finally, in mid-April 2007 the *Wall Street Journal* published a long article about the growth of militant, evangelistic atheism in Europe. Atheism in Europe is nothing new, but what is new is that European atheists, like the American scientists at the Scripps Institute forum reported by the *New York Times,* consider it necessary to compete with religion for public support, as if they are more desperate than confident, no longer feeling that they can assume that the war has ended and they have won. For me the importance of this news is that university teachers around the world must also wake up to the fact that there is no group of experts which has uncontested authority to decide what is real. Universities must and will give serious consideration to the positive case for atheism, which means that the atheists will for the first time have to defend a position rather than merely take skeptical shots at Christianity, and the Christians will sometimes enjoy the luxury of taking the skeptical position.

This brings us to the question of liberation. Dawkins and Dennet seem to think that the American and British people live in an age of theocratic oppression, from which they will want to escape if they are shown that escape is possible. I argue that the true oppressor in our time is scientific naturalism, a philosophy that has become dominant in culture and government because eloquent representatives of the scientific establishment have taught us that to believe that the success of science in providing technology is tied to the worldview of naturalism, so that any questioning of the worldview endangers the continuance of the technology. This identification of scientific technology with the dominance of naturalism as a worldview is a very vulnerable thesis, and the fact that highly visible popularizers of science have turned from implicit to explicit advocacy of atheism may provide logical thinkers with the opportunity to show that the alleged connection does not exist.

2

HARVARD'S ABORTED REQUIREMENT IN REASON AND FAITH

Phillip E. Johnson

Because our primary concern in this book is to explore how the issues raised by the new wave of scientific atheism can and should be addressed in higher education and scholarship, I was particularly interested when I came upon an opinion article by the passionately Darwinist Harvard psychology professor and popular author Steven Pinker. This article was published online in late October 2006 in the *Harvard Crimson,* Harvard's student-edited daily newspaper, and revealed that the Harvard faculty was seriously considering requiring a course in the relationship of faith to reason.

Pinker is not one of the scientific atheists who were interviewed for the November 2006 *Wired* cover article, but he is very definitely in the Dawkins camp, as evidenced by his own books and his enthusiastic jacket endorsement for Richard Dawkins's book *The God Delusion.* Pinker's article criticized a report by the Harvard faculty's Committee on General Education, which had proposed that Harvard's required general education curriculum should be expanded to include a course in "Science and Technology" and another in "Reason and Faith."

Pinker began with some polite generalities before launching into his substantive criticisms of the report's two main proposals. He thought that the science and technology requirement aimed too low by focusing on only the uses to which scientific technology has been put, some positive and others negative. "Missing from the report," Pinker wrote, was a "sensitivity to the ennobling nature of scientific knowledge: to the inherent value of understanding how the world works, the history of life and our planet, the forces that make it tick, the stuff we're made of, the origin of living things, and the machinery of life, including our own mental life." To illustrate his point, Pinker specified some particularly important items of scientific knowledge:

1. "for example, that our planet is an undistinguished speck in an inconceivably vast cosmos" (recall from chap. 1 the description of Dr. Carolyn Porco's photograph of a gigantic Saturn with a barely visible earth in the background)

2. "that all the hope and ingenuity in the world can't create energy or use it without loss"

3. "that our species has existed for only a tiny fraction of the history of the earth"

4. "that humans are primates"

5. "that the mind is the activity of an organ that runs by physiological processes" (Dr. Pinker did not say whether

the mind and its thoughts, including his own thoughts, are nothing but the product of such physiochemical processes. If that were the case, we would have to wonder whether our vaunted rationality is an illusion produced by brain chemistry.)

6. "that there are methods of ascertaining the truth that can force us to conclusions which violate common sense, sometimes radically so, at scales very large and very small" (Apparently, Dr. Pinker here was referring to relativity [very large scale] and quantum mechanics [very small scale]. Both of these theories violate common sense expectations, although physicists find them to be very satisfactory, and indispensable for their research.)

7. "that precious and widely held beliefs, when subjected to empirical tests, are often cruelly falsified" (I infer that Dr. Pinker was referring to religious beliefs, and especially to matters taught in the Bible. He did not say whether there are any precious and widely held scientific beliefs of our time, such as the belief that a combination of random genetic mutations has the ability to create new complex forms of living organisms that might be cruelly falsified if required to pass experimental tests.)

Pinker wrapped up his list of essential scientific doctrines by saying "I believe that a person for whom this understanding is not second-nature cannot be said to be educated." To say that a scientific understanding has become second nature is to say that it has become absorbed into common sense, but one of the understandings that must become second nature is that commonsense beliefs may be cruelly falsified, if they are subjected to rigorous scientific testing, rather than being complacently protected as part of what "everybody knows."

Pinker saved his heaviest critical artillery for the "reason and faith" requirement, of which he disapproved in principle. He defined faith as a euphemism for religious belief and as meaning believing something (such as that God exists) without good reasons to do so. He did not consider the possibility that there might be good reasons for believing that God exists, although there have been many esteemed philosophers, and even scientists, who thought so. So defined, Dr. Pinker suspected that the proposed requirement placed superstition on the same level as reason as two parallel and equivalent ways of pursuing knowledge. This contrived intellectual equivalence was wrong, he said, because a university should be devoted to reason only. Faith has no place in anything but a religious institution and not at a temple of reason like Harvard. To Pinker, it was as if the committee was proposing a requirement for students to study astrology along with astronomy, or alchemy with chemistry. If the proposed requirement was based on an assumption that religious differences are responsible for contemporary conflicts, then the subject should be left to courses in international politics, where professors could decide in specific instances whether or not religion was an important factor, without having the judgment made for them by a course title in a curriculum.

Dr. Pinker concluded his essay by observing that

> we [Harvard's faculty] have to keep in mind that the requirement will attract attention far and wide, and for a long time. For us to magnify the significance of religion as a topic equivalent in scope to all of science, all of culture, or all of

world history and current affairs, is to give it far too much prominence. It is an American anachronism, I think, in an era in which the rest of the West is moving beyond it.

Pinker did not find it necessary to mention the global East or South. He seemed to assume, as many American intellectuals do, that Western Europe sets the cultural gold standard to which the rest of the world should aspire.

The Harvard faculty committee was apparently persuaded by Professor Pinker's arguments, because I read in the *Boston Globe* a few days later that the committee had rescinded its proposal that students take what the *Globe* called "a class dealing with religion." In place of its original proposal the committee now proposed a course in "What it means to be a human being." The revised requirement, according to the *Globe*'s Harvard source, will "encompass religious thought, art, literature, and philosophy, as well as evolutionary biology and cognitive science." I noted the absence of that red-flag word *faith*.

The chairwoman of the general education task force claimed that her group did not make the switch because of objections to the topic. Rather, she said they were convinced by their colleagues that the same issues could be adequately covered in other categories, including moral reasoning and requirements covering society in the United States and abroad (which was exactly what Professor Pinker had proposed). The newspaper commented that the switch was sure to disappoint some people both inside and outside Harvard who had been excited to see the subject of religion elevated to an important place in the curriculum. What amazed me about the entire episode was not that the proposal was defeated but that there are Harvard faculty insiders who want to elevate religion or faith, if these are not two words for the same thing, to an important place in Harvard's curriculum. That the attempt was made and got as far as it did may be more important than that it did not succeed on the first attempt, following a century or more of casually assumed agnosticism.

One professor, identified in the newspaper by the pejorative (at Harvard) label "conservative," commented that "I think secular and liberal Harvard rebelled." That may be a fair description of what happened, but the rebellion may not make very much difference in the end. Whether we were created by God or by a purposeless nature, whatever the time scale, certainly has relevance for what it means to be human, and we can reasonably expect that Harvard students will be discussing the God question and the adequacy of scientific materialism as a worldview in their dormitories and their dining rooms. In fact, Professor Pinker's essay might make a good framework for such discussions, in or out of the classroom, provided that his statements are considered not as preconditions for discussion, as he seems to have intended, but as provocative opinions to be examined and analyzed. (The opinions we express in this book should also be taken that way. Our aim is to propose an agenda for discussion rather than to settle the issues at once.) If I had the honor to be a member of the Harvard faculty, I might have suggested that the proposed course be titled "Reason and Scientific Materialism." I suppose that scientific materialists on the faculty might not have objected to giving their own views such prominence, yet the title would open the classroom to discussing the possibility that reason and materialism are not the same thing.

Eventually, some Harvard professors will want to bring discussions of fundamental issues into the classroom. This will probably happen gradually and informally rather than all at once in response to a master plan, but that may be for the best. We do know that there is substantial Christian consciousness and activity among Harvard students, and it is not because the students have been indoctrinated by their parents, but because they came to Harvard and discovered that the university, for all its excellence, is lacking something important, both spiritually and intellectually. A recent dean of Harvard College has published a book about Harvard's undergraduate college titled *Excellence Without a Soul,* and many others have also noticed that something important is missing from the Harvard package.

To learn more about the Christian renaissance among Harvard students, I recommend reading *Finding God Beyond Harvard* by Kelly Monroe Kullberg. Ms. Kullberg is a charming and dynamic young woman who came to the Harvard Divinity School in the late 1980s (perhaps the last place in America where anyone would expect to find God) and stayed to found a sensationally successful guest lecture series called the Veritas Forum ("Veritas" [truth] is Harvard's motto). The lecture series, aimed at challenging Harvard's intellectuals to consider the rationality of Christian truth claims, grew into a way of life for the many students and staff who participated, and inspired imitators throughout the nation. Perhaps Pinker's protest was sparked by a concern that the issues raised by the Veritas Forum might gain legitimacy as a component in Harvard's curriculum.

I think it would have been a good idea for Harvard to have included a "reason and faith" requirement in its general education requirement, because this relationship is an important subject for any liberal education, and it does not merely designate a "course dealing with religion" as the *Boston Globe* mistakenly supposed.

Naturalistic rationalists like Steven Pinker typically begin any discussion of faith and reason by oversimplifying the subject in two ways. First, they identify "faith" with religion, thus wrongly assuming that the only faith of any importance is faith in a supernatural being (God). Because these rationalists assume that reason by definition rejects the existence of any supernatural being, to them such faith is by definition irrational, and faith so defined cannot be taken seriously in a community dedicated to reason, although it can be studied in the same sense that madness or ignorance can be studied, presumably with a view to alleviating the affliction.

For a very different understanding of faith, consider the explanation given by C. S. Lewis in *Mere Christianity*. To Lewis, having faith means not believing something without good reasons, but retaining confidence in what you have good reason to believe when you are in danger of becoming confused and losing your bearings. Lewis gives an example from ordinary life. A boy learning to swim knows perfectly well that an unsupported body will not necessarily sink in water; he has seen dozens of people float and swim. But the whole question is whether he will be able to go on believing this when the instructor takes away his hand and leaves him unsupported in the water—or whether he will suddenly cease to believe it, get in a fright and go down. Many examples could be drawn from the realm of athletics. Athletes must have faith that the techniques they have practiced will prove sound in the stress of competition. A figure skater who allows doubt to enter his or her mind is likely to fall, and a basketball player who adopts a new shooting style during a game is unlikely to score. Among golfers, the necessity of having faith in one's swing is proverbial. On the practice tee the golfer experiments, but once the golfer is in tournament play and committed to a shot, he or she thinks only positive thoughts.

Scientists in particular have to be men or women of faith. Scientific research is a difficult and frequently discouraging enterprise in which success often comes, if at all, only after repeated failures. To be successful, scientists have to learn not to allow difficulties to destroy their confidence that success can eventually be achieved. This is faith of a kind, but in principle it is rational, because scientists know that scientists of the past have sometimes achieved success only after long years of frustration, when they were repeatedly tempted to give up and admit failure. History teaches us that it is often reasonable to have faith in the ability of scientists to achieve seemingly impossible goals, and sometimes unreasonable to scoff at such faith. Yet there is a limit. Sometimes repeated failure is a sign that reaching a goal by the means one has been using truly is impossible, and to ignore that sign is madness, not faith.

Alchemists had faith that they could transform base metals to gold, but their persistence after lifetimes of failure made them seem ridiculous rather than heroic. I sometimes think of alchemy when reading of the constantly unsuccessful efforts of modern scientists to determine how nonliving chemicals combined by natural means on the early Earth to form the first living cells. To keep going, naturalistic scientists have to have faith that this seeming chemical miracle actually did occur through some rare combination of chance and chemical law, because their guiding philosophy teaches them that otherwise the long process of biological evolution could never have begun, and we would not be here to ponder the problem. Evolutionary scientists fiercely resist my suggestion that the transformation from lifeless chemicals to living cell may have required the participation of intelligence, because it seems that the intelligence would have to be supernatural, there being no human chemists or laboratories on earth at the time. The suggestion of intelligent cause then amounts to creationism, which they consider to be a betrayal of science. Who is more rational, the scientist who clings to his or her faith, or the legal scholar (me) who tries to unsettle that faith by citing evidence and a record of experimental failure.

If I were planning a course in reason and faith, the first thing I would want my students to understand is that it is wrong to assume that some people (e.g., the ones you find in church) rely on faith, whereas other people (e.g., the ones you would find in a laboratory) rely solely on reason. It would be much closer to the truth to say that everybody relies on faith and everybody reasons. For example, many scientists today have an absolute faith in naturalism. Naturalism in this context is a philosophical doctrine that says that our universe is a closed system of natural causes and effects. On this assumption every natural phenomenon, like the origin of life, for example, is securely known to be explicable on the basis of natural causes accessible to scientific investigation—some combination of chemical laws and chance, to be more specific. Scientific rationalists consider that the many successes of science fully justify them in holding this faith with absolute certainty. Indeed, they consider that faith in scientific naturalism is so thoroughly justified by reason that they do not think of it as a faith but as a defining example of reason. The truth is that having the right kind of faith is not an alternative to reason, but an essential element of reason. That is why we can say to one another in argument, "You are not wrong to have faith, but you ought to place your faith in something more worthy." Communists had faith that their system would ultimately prevail despite its defects, because they had convinced themselves that history was on their side. They were not wrong to have faith, but they should have placed their faith in something more worthy.

A positive example to consider would be the faith of Winston Churchill in 1940. To impartial observers, including several members of Churchill's war cabinet, the Germans had effectively won the war once they had broken through the French lines. From that position the way was open for the Nazis to occupy Paris and even to surround and capture the British army in France. Pointing out that further fighting would only lead to further defeats, the Peace Party in the British government argued that the rational action was to negotiate for peace.

Churchill refused to consider negotiation and insisted that the British would fight to the bitter end, no matter what the outcome might be. To the Peace Party this intransigence seemed irrational and showed only that Churchill was refusing to recognize reality. Since Britain would have to come to terms with a victorious Hitler in the end, the way to get the best terms in a peace treaty was to negotiate while Britain still had an army in the field and thus had a position from which to negotiate.

In this dispute Churchill was the man of faith who refused to acknowledge that defeat was unavoidable, even though the circumstances, considered objectively, were extremely unfavorable. In hindsight we know that Churchill was right, because it turned out that German might was not as irresistible as it seemed, and new circumstances, unforeseeable in 1940, led to the entry of Russia and the United States into the war against Hitler in 1941. This is only one of many instances where the person of faith was able to change history. Another example for students to consider would be Abraham Lincoln at the most discouraging moments during the American Civil War, when it seemed that victory could not be achieved.

For one fictional example, think of J. R. R. Tolkien's *Return of the King,* when the beleaguered army stormed the Dark Gate with the hope that they might create a distraction that would allow Frodo to reach the Mount of Doom with the Ring of Power. Reason would have dictated despair; faith brought victory. For another example from literature, Shakespeare's Othello had every reason to believe that his wife Desdemona was faithful to him. But because he lacked sufficient faith in her virtue, the cunning Iago was able to convince him with faked proofs that she was having an affair with another man. It was not so much that Othello lacked faith but that he placed his faith in the honesty of Iago rather than in his wife's loyalty. Like the communists mentioned earlier, he placed his faith in an unworthy object, so acted unreasonably.

Faith and religion are not the same thing; neither are reason and science (or logic). There is such a thing as reasonable faith and unreasonable science or logic. Paranoids, for example, are highly logical. It is just that they start from the misperception that they are the center of the world's attention. Faith is a component of reason. We reason from principles. Even our adherence to logic is faith.

Students should be encouraged to think about the part that faith plays in their own lives. We don't start over each day; we have faith in people and events that we have come to trust. Our experiences are important in determining how we live. Dawkins views (has faith in) the world as morally arbitrary, but there are reasons to think that this is not so. Two great tyrannies that dominated Europe in 1939 eventually perished from the consequences of their own excesses, although not without doing a great deal of damage first.

3

EARTH'S DISTINCTION

Phillip E. Johnson

The first item on Harvard professor Steven Pinker's list of essential items of scientific knowledge (see pp. 26-27) is that "our planet is an undistinguished speck in an inconceivably vast cosmos." Pinker's statement seems based on the premise that size is what matters in planets, in which case a mere speck is by definition unimportant. But perhaps a very small planet can in some important respects be more distinguished than a huge one.

To be sure, Earth is small compared to a giant planet like Saturn, with its glorious rings. On the other hand, Earth does have something that Saturn lacks, namely, a protective atmosphere suitable for harboring life, and a multitude of complex plants and animals, including humans, with our artistic and technological achievements, which include a program of space exploration that allows us to admire Saturn by close-up color photos. That point leads to the question addressed in this chapter. Are the earth's life-friendly qualities unique, or at least rare, or are there millions of similar planets harboring complex life forms and technologically advanced civilizations elsewhere in the universe? In the recent as well as the distant past, imaginative people have thought the existence of intelligent beings and advanced civilizations on other planets to be highly probable, as some people still do. Early in the twentieth century some astronomers reported seeing canals on the surface of Mars, which implied the existence of a civilization capable of building and maintaining a canal network.

The widespread notion that civilization existed on Mars made it possible for Orson Welles to create a public panic in America with his notorious "War of the Worlds" radio broadcast in 1938. When I was a boy I remember imaginative people believing that the clouds covering Venus signaled the existence of rain forests underneath, which presumably teemed with life just as rain forests do on earth. It was a great disappointment to learn from better observations that Venus has a poisonous atmosphere and a surface temperature inconsistent with the presence of life. Scientists still think it possible that Mars may once have harbored microbial life, and that the same is also possible for Titan, Saturn's largest satellite. While I (Johnson) was writing this chapter, NASA scientists announced, on August 1, 2008, that the Phoenix Mars lander had confirmed the existence of frozen water under the surface of Mars. News reports speculated that the discovery of water might soon be followed by the discovery of microbial life on Mars. If life of any sort is found on Mars, that will be very interesting. If no life is found, despite the presence of water and the necessary chemicals, that will be even more interesting. I predict that, while something that the scientists agree to call "life" may be found, there will no cellular life as we know it on Earth, with its complex protein construction machinery. That requires not just water and favorable conditions, but also a designer. The risk of falsification that concerns me is not that cellular life will evolve without a designer, but that the designer may have been active on more than one planet. If life is found on Mars, the materialists who dominate biology will regard its mere existence as proof that no designer was needed for the origin of life on either Mars or Earth.

No one expects any longer to find complex life or civilization on any planet in our solar system, except on Earth. All hopes for finding intelligent life on any other planet now rest on the radio telescopes of the SETI (Search for Extraterrestrial Intelligence) Project, which scan the skies in hope of detecting radio signals that carry a message from some technologically advanced civilization light-years away that is trying to communicate with us. The same scientists that think extraterrestrial intelligent beings exist also think these beings will desire to communicate with us, just as we wish to communicate with them. That we have not found their signals proves only that we have not searched long enough or in the right places. After much dedicated searching, SETI has not received any message. Radio signals abound, but, on close examination, so far they have all been products of natural (unintelligent) physical causes rather than messages from an intelligent sender.

Many of the current SETI enthusiasts were fans of the 1960s television series *Star Trek*, on which the admirable Captain James Kirk and his intrepid crew piloted their starship *Enterprise* on a thorough exploration of our galaxy, in each episode finding a new inhabited planet to which they could "beam down" for a battle of wits with the inhabitants. These aliens often behaved in ways that seemed strange to an earthling, but they were physically very much like Earth's people, who in turn had no difficulty breathing their planets' atmospheres. *Star Trek* was a captivating scientific myth of the twentieth century and is probably largely responsible for the fact that hope of finding technologically advanced civilization elsewhere in the universe dies hard. Persons who have imaginatively explored the galaxy in their youth and found it to be full of fascinating civilizations are very naturally inclined to believe that alien civilizations exist, and if they are spending their careers trying to contact the aliens, the incentive to believe must be enormous. Since many of these intelligent aliens may have been evolving for a much longer time than we have, it is likely that they will possess knowledge and wisdom much greater than ours and can become our tutors to guide us through the perilous times ahead. In *The Selfish Gene*, Richard Dawkins speculated that if superintelligent aliens discover our planet, the first question they will ask about us is, "Have they found out about evolution yet?" That humbling question should finally put an end to the puzzling persistence of skepticism about Darwinism! Dawkins does not bother to consider that his hypothetical superior aliens might ask if the Creator has revealed himself to us.

If we turn from fantasy and speculation to science, however, we quickly find that there is no evidence that intelligent life, superior to us or not, exists anywhere but on our own planet. An alien civilization, if any exists, might yet contact us, but reason requires that we seriously consider the possibility that science and civilization exist only on Earth. It is true that some people claim, with apparent sincerity, to have been abducted by aliens and taken away for a time in alien spaceships for scientific experiments. A Harvard psychiatry professor gained notoriety by announcing that he believed some of these claims of alien abductions. Perhaps he reasoned that if it is reasonable to believe in the aliens, as many scientists do, then it is also reasonable to believe in the abductions. It would be more consistent with a scientific outlook to be skeptical about the existence of the aliens, as well as the abductions.

Faith in the existence of life on other planets would have been an excellent subject for discussion in that proposed Harvard class on reason and faith (see chap. 2). On the basis of all the evidence we have today, there is little reason for believing that intelligent life exists anywhere except on Earth. There are not any planets that are reasonable candidates for bearers of complex, multicellular life. Some planets have been detected in orbit around distant stars, but most are extremely non-Earthlike, being gas giants like Jupiter, with orbits that keep them either too far from or too close to their sun for water to exist in liquid form. It may be conceivable that some very exotic form of life can thrive on a gas giant, and even that it is in some sense intelligent, but there is no evidence that such life exists and much reason to believe it does not. More recently, the discovery of a few rocky planets at a distance from a star that might allow a temperature suitable for liquid water has sparked renewed excitement about the possibility of extraterrestrial life, but the existence of either the water or the life, especially civilized life, is still entirely hypothetical.

It is reasonable to assume tentatively, then, when discussing the importance of Earth in the cosmos, that intelligent life exists only on this planet and has never existed anywhere else. If new evidence appears of the present or past existence of intelligent life elsewhere in the universe, then it will be necessary to reconsider that assumption, but until then the evidence supports the view that Earth is very distinguished indeed as the only location in the entire cosmos where intelligent life, and perhaps even much simpler life, exists now or even in the past. Granted the premise, how great is the distinction? I once read a materialist's argument that the presence of intelligent life seems important to us because we belong to an intelligent species, and are concerned to magnify our importance. Who are we to say that our humble lives are more important than Saturn's glorious rings or Titan's rivers of methane? I acknowledge that if there were people on Titan, their point of view would be as worthy of respect as ours. It seems, however, Saturn and Titan are lifeless. A lifeless piece of rock, however large and rich in chemicals, cannot have a point of view. If our point of view is the only one in existence, then, self-glorifying or not, it faces no competition.

If our tentative conclusion is correct, then to what do we owe Earth's distinction as the sole place in the cosmos where intelligent life exists? One answer could be chance. Another answer might be that there is a cosmic designer—call it God—who designed this one planet as uniquely suitable for complex life and prepared it as a home for a uniquely intelligent creature with whom God might have fellowship. I am sure that one of today's Darwinian scientists, educated from an early age to understand science as committed by definition to a naturalistic worldview, would insist that the former possibility (chance) is the only possibility, because terrible things will happen if that designer, whatever it is called, is allowed to take up residence in science, where we decide what is real and what is not. Within the confines of this book, however, we feel free to consider all reasonable possibilities, because here there are no secular pressure groups or federal judges (I hope) who can appear and order us to consider only the options approved by scientific materialists.

In that spirit I propose that at this point we recess for a brief consideration of an important book, *Privileged Planet: How Our Planet Is Designed for Discovery*, by astronomer Guillermo Gonzalez and philosopher Jay Richards (available with an accompanying DVD that summarizes the argument of the book in the form of an illustrated lecture). Gonzalez and Richards describe how Earth is uniquely favored with conditions that not only allow the survival of a species such as ours, but that also make it possible for our scientists to make discoveries about the universe. It is as if a designer of the cosmos wanted to prepare all things to not only make possible our existence but also encourage us to learn about the cosmos through scientific investigation.

I am sufficiently naive to have hoped that a designer of this sort would be tolerated by scientific organizations, since the concept confers a divine blessing on science. This optimism failed to take into account the knee-jerk outrage with which big science greets any suggestion that the cosmos might be rooted in reason, even if it is a reason that highly values science. When the staff of the Smithsonian Institution's Museum of Natural History in Washington, D.C., scheduled a showing of the *Privileged Planet* DVD, protests were organized, journalistic allies were summoned, and the public was warned that the sky would fall if the video were not repudiated. The governors of the Institution duly disclaimed responsibility but allowed the showing to take place after downgrading the status of the event. The backlash continued subsequently, when demonstrations were organized against Gonzalez at his home campus, to show that heresy in science does not go unpunished.

Subsequently Gonzalez was denied promotion to tenure rank at Iowa State University, despite a superior record of teaching and publication. If science exists on other planets, perhaps Earth still has the distinction of being the only planet where science is required to be virulently hostile to any departure from materialist orthodoxy.

If indeed Earth is the only place with civilized life or even life of any kind, what does this say about the importance of our planet in a universe containing trillions of stars? Is this life only on one planet out of so many in the cosmos the result of natural causes, or does it signal the existence of a creator, who chose to distinguish the Earth in this fashion? What bearing does this have on the Darwinist doctrine that life arose on the Earth by natural causes and then progressed to its present complexity and diversity by random variation and natural selection? If natural causes can create the enormously complex and diverse organisms we see around us on Earth, then shouldn't they have done so on many other planets as well?

Scientific rationalists can argue that merely casting doubt on the ability of natural causes to produce complex life does not necessarily mean that any other explanation is correct. There would still be other arguments against the existence of a beneficial, supernatural creator, including the existence of much undeserved pain and suffering. This line of argument is certainly an appropriate subject for classroom consideration in the context of other subjects in this chapter. How might a Christian theist respond to this concern?

Young people in a class examining these questions could be assigned to watch some of the many programs about exploration of the universe. The assignments would be to note how much emphasis is placed on finding life elsewhere, also to listen carefully to what is said and note down how much of it is speculation. Then it would be good to learn more about what makes the Earth specially fitted for life. As they learn more about the many conditions that have to be just right, it will help them to think more clearly about the larger questions. Does the vastness of the cosmos argue for theism or against it? Is Earth special? Is humanity?

Pinker has raised the right questions, but the answers will be as much about philosophic assumptions as they are about scientific evidence. Students should be allowed to hear the perspectives of theists and of nontheists in a fair and open manner during class. If Pinker's philosophy is represented, then so should arguments of theistic philosophers and scientists who disagree.

This open dialogue will not guarantee students take any particular perspective, but will make for a better education.

4

THE DARWINIAN WORLDVIEW

Phillip E. Johnson

Darwinism may refer either to a specific theory of biology or
to an episteme, a way of thinking about things in general. In
explaining why we should believe that there is no God, Richard Dawkins placed particular importance on the power of
the theory of natural selection to act as a consciousness
raiser, alerting our minds to a way of thinking that is appli-
cable to many subjects outside of biology. "Natural selection
not only explains the whole of life," wrote Dawkins, "it also
raises our consciousness to the power of science to explain
how organized complexity can emerge from simple begin-
nings without deliberate guidance."[1] In that formulation, belief in the biological theory comes first. The biological theory,
understood, raises our consciousness to the power of science
to explain everything by natural causes. Thus, belief in theory comes first, and the raised consciousness, with its re-

---

[1] Richard Dawkins, *The God Delusion* (New York: Houghton Mifflin Harcourt,
2006), p. 116.

formed episteme, follows thereafter. It might be more illuminating, however, to consider that in some cases the sequence may be reversed.

When teaching the theory of evolution, students must be taught first to approach the subject in the correct (naturalistic) manner, for otherwise the instructor may encounter resistance. The students must be taught that science is the supreme judge of what is reasonable and what is not, and that the world, as seen by science, is composed only of material entities that act on each other according to physical laws or chance. The teacher may concede that scientific knowledge is currently incomplete and therefore some difficult questions are not yet adequately answered. What is securely known is that evolution employed only natural causes, like chance and physical laws. To imagine that evolution is guided by an unevolved intelligence is futile and foolish. If this preparation is done correctly, then these students' consciousness will be sufficiently raised that the naturalistic theory of evolution will seem not only believable but inevitable. They will have been trained to think as metaphysical materialists or physicalists. Intelligence may play a role only after it has itself evolved by natural, material causes, as human beings are presumed to have done. That is why Darwinian evolution is a theory of importance to biologists, but it is also much more than that. Once fully assimilated, it frees (or forces) the mind to understand everything in a new light.

The effect on the materialist believer is often similar to a religious conversion, just as was a conversion to Freudianism or Marxism in the days when these philosophies were esteemed as sciences. In some cases a Christian who accepts the Darwinian episteme may convert directly to atheism. In other cases the Christian may become a theistic evolutionist and thereafter defend Darwinism as tenaciously as Dawkins himself, but insisting that the theory is fully consistent with an orthodox Christian faith and even saying that it is heretical or even "blasphemous" for other Christians to deny that all species, including humans, evolved by a purely natural process that was not guided by God. Theistic evolutionists do not see their position as self-contradictory. They see themselves as accepting "good science" but declining to apply the Darwinist episteme outside its home territory in biology. I suspect that a later generation will study Darwinism and grasp the main point: if there is no place for God in the world that science studies, then there is no place for God in reality.

To illustrate the broad applicability of Darwinian theory, Dawkins cited a physicist who reportedly said that modern cosmology began with Charles Darwin and Alfred Russell Wallace, the codiscoverers of the biological theory of natural selection, because these men were the first to supply an explanation for our existence that excluded any role for a supernatural agent. That is a good, succinct statement of the central point of Darwin's theory. If it is true, the theory explains our existence without allowing any role for a supernatural agent (e.g., God). (In fact, Wallace exasperated Darwin by leaving the door open for God to reenter biology when he argued that natural selection could not explain human higher mental faculties.) Darwin's theory makes the existence of a supernatural creator superfluous because the theory tells us that nature can and did accomplish the creating without any help. Theistic evolutionists such as Francis Collins attempt to separate the Darwinian episteme from its theory of biology, fiercely defending the latter while struggling to confine the former to so narrow a range that the theistic evolutionist can still think as a creationist about any subject other than biology. Thus in chapter one, we saw how Francis Collins, unwilling to abandon science altogether to the materialists, sought to find a place for God as the agent responsible for fine-tuning the fundamental constants of physics so as to make the existence of life possible. Like Richard Dawkins, I see this retreat from biology into physics as an unfortunate maneuver that fails to explain how it can be logically consistent for a biologist to insist on employing only naturalistic reasoning in biology and then employ theistic reasoning in physics.

Eventually, the Darwinist whose consciousness has been sufficiently raised realizes that the logical thing to do is not to attempt to comprehend Darwinism from a Christian episteme, but rather to confine Christian belief within a Darwinian episteme, which excludes from reality any role for a supernatural agent (such as God). When the inquiry is directed that way, the question is not whether Christian belief is true, because that possibility is excluded by definition, unless Christian belief can survive the amputation of all its supernatural elements.

The consistent Darwinist is interested only in how inclination to religious belief arose in human history as a consequence of random genetic variation and survived, because under primitive conditions, those who had the gene for belief tended to outbreed those who lacked it. This Darwinian story is consistent with the possibility that the "god gene," under modern conditions, threatens the survival of the species, and so it urgently needs to be deactivated or confined.

I appreciate the consistency of Dawkins's logic at this

point. If natural selection really does explain the whole of life, then we should expect it to explain the entire scope of life, including human behavior and human beliefs about God or anything else. That explains why it is impossible to kill off social Darwinism, regardless of how many follies or crimes have been committed in its name. The substance of social Darwinism eventually returns under a new name and attains renewed respectability, because it is still firmly based in the greater Darwinism. I use the term "greater Darwinism" to refer to the Darwinian worldview that results from a fully raised consciousness, by analogy to the way we refer to a large urban area that surrounds a relatively compact central city.

The debate between Francis Collins and Richard Dawkins reported in chapter one illustrates the difference between Darwinism as a scientific theory and Darwinism as an episteme or way of thinking about everything. Francis Collins accepts and enthusiastically defends all the scientific claims of Darwinism, but then attempts to force the theory into a Christian episteme by reaching for a scientific foundation for God in cosmology. Of course, this makes Francis Collins a potential ally in shaking naturalism's confidence that science can explain everything.

Judged from the Darwinian episteme, Collins has not had his consciousness raised enough by the study of Darwinism, and so although Collins's biology is orthodox, he is missing the point of the theory. He bravely tries to squeeze Darwinism into a Christian worldview. This is barely possible, as long as the Christian deals only with the biological theory and ignores the episteme. However, as Daniel Dennett famously wrote in *Darwin's Dangerous Idea*, Darwinism, fully assimilated, is a kind of philosophical "universal acid" that eats away just about every traditional concept and leaves in its wake a revolutionized worldview. One thinker after another has tried to find some way to contain this acid in order to protect something from its corrosive force. But the defining characteristic of universal acid is that it eats away everything, including the container that was meant to hold it.

Dawkins's book-length atheist manifesto—*The God Delusion*—is ambitious and daring. We admire it for those qualities, and think it understandable that Dawkins's way of thinking is attracting an enormous amount of attention, even (or perhaps especially) in a nation that is at least nominally overwhelmingly Christian. The very preponderance of Christians in America creates a defensive reaction among unbelievers. There is such a tradition of this that if you come upon the Skeptics Society or a magazine titled *Skeptical Enquirer*, it is a safe bet that the skepticism will be directed at the existence of God or some other element of Christian belief. "Skeptics" are not skeptical of scientific materialism or any of the cherished doctrines of the current scientific establishment which are taught as unshakeable truth from elementary school to doctoral studies. If we consider the naturalistic worldview that rules contemporary education at all levels to be the orthodoxy, then the Christians should be termed the true skeptics, rather than the natural target of skepticism.

On April 15, 2007, the *New York Times* published an opinion column by the brilliant, conservative-leaning writer David Brooks headlined "The Age of Darwin." Beginning with a polite bow to postmodernist fashion, Brooks observed that most historians today hate grand unifying narratives, which carry an accompanying assumption that history is the march of progress upward to its fulfillment in the present. Quickly changing direction, Brooks next announced that "while 'we' postmoderns say we detest all-explaining grand narratives, in fact a newish grand narrative has crept upon us willy-nilly and is now all around us. Once the Bible shaped all conversation, then Marx, then Freud, but today Darwin is everywhere." Brooks was evidently referring not to Darwin's original theory of how favorable variations spread through a preexisting population, but to the ambitious gene-centered Darwinian worldview that has spread widely through the intelligentsia through the books of Richard Dawkins and his allies.

"Scarcely a month goes by," Brooks continued,

> when Time or Newsweek doesn't have a cover article on how our genes shape everything from our exercise habits to our moods. . . . Neuroscientists debate the existence of God on the best-seller lists, while evolutionary theory reshapes psychology, dieting and literary criticism. Confident and exhilarated, evolutionary theorists believe they have a universal framework to explain human behavior.

That's true enough, but it may be a little misleading to say that neuroscientists debate the existence of God. They may occasionally do that; however, they typically do not debate God's existence but rather supply a genetic explanation for his existence in terms of brain chemistry for why people believe in God or anything else. The one subject to which the corrosive Darwinian method is never applied is Darwinism itself, which is too cherished to be subjected to such undignified investigation. It must be a rock of certainty, while everything else is dissolved into shifting sand by the acid of reductionism. In consequence, the possibility that Darwinism itself is a product of brain chemistry rather than reason is never mentioned, much less featured on the cover of *Time*.

When you hold a dominating position of unquestioned epistemic superiority, you do not need to debate rivals on equal terms, because it is safer and more devastating to sweep them away by explaining them in the language of your own paradigm. Freudians used to do the same thing. When Freud took the role of the scientist and cast his readers as so many objects of scientific study, then any reader's refusal to believe Freud's theory manifested an unwillingness to face the truth, and persons in "denial" of reality could only be helped by psychoanalytic therapy. Freud wrote a famous book titled *The Future of an Illusion,* putting religious believers on the couch and predicting the coming disappearance of God's illusory existence as more and more people learned from mind scientists like Freud how the illusion was produced. I remember being assigned this book in college. This was only a generation before the scientific pretensions of Freudianism were themselves exposed as illusory, and the theory lost its power over the minds of all but a tiny band of diehard disciples. It turned out that the "illusion" of Freud's title was his own theory. Now, like the Marxists and Freudians before them, the Darwinians are convinced that they have a theory of everything human, which gives them a power denied to those who have not been taught the great theory or who refuse to believe it. The examples of Marx and Freud show that a theory which is all-powerful in one generation can lose all its magic in the next. Sam Harris wrote *The End of Faith.* Perhaps the Darwinian metanarrative will come to an end instead.

A little more than two weeks after the Brooks essay appeared online, on May 2, the *New York Times* reported that, across the United States, at universities as varied as Harvard; the University of Wisconsin, Madison; and the University of California, Berkeley, where I reside, students are being drawn to religion with more fervor than at any time observers can remember. Although the kind of religion was not specified in the story, the context made clear that it is mostly evangelical Christianity, as taught on campus by parachurch groups like InterVarsity Christian Fellowship. One does not find such groups featured on the cover of *Time* or *Newsweek*, but the college students of today will make up the intellectual leaders of the next generation. Clearly, we live in an interesting time. On the one hand, we have a dominant materialist metanarrative constantly being expanded by its supporters, who are confident in their power to explain everything human, including religious belief, as a product of material causes like DNA or brain chemistry. Some of the most publicly visible scientists are throwing caution to the winds and urging the public not only to cease believing in God but also to cease granting respect or tolerance to those who do believe. On the other hand, we have a generation of students at our best universities who are more committed to Christian faith than at any time in living memory. What will happen after these students graduate and move into scientific positions, college professorships or even influential positions in journalism? Will they become socialized to a secularized, agnostic worldview in order to get along with their elders, or will they retain their faith and with it change the culture of America and the world?

The question of "getting along" is a serious one for young

scholars. Darwinism validates the authority of a certain cultural elite, and they will be reluctant to allow any questioning of that authority. They feel a sense of superiority because they know the "true story" of how we came to be. They can lecture the masses on that story. Because it is the central story or who we are, they also believe they have the authority to tell us where we are going and how we should behave. Anyone who questions their "true story" is marginalized, and career and social problems may result.

Because my crystal ball is as clouded as everyone else's, I won't try to pick a winner at this early date. All I will say is that it *is* an early date, and we must keep in mind that experts who try to predict what the world will be like a generation or two later are frequently far off track. What I like about today's new atheists is that while they may have the wrong answer, they are focusing attention on the right question. Is God real or imaginary? In my student days the experts were all predicting that the world would inevitably be secularized as its people grew steadily more accustomed to relying on modern technology. That has not happened. Today it seems that faith in God is at least as energetic now as it was a century ago, not only in parts of the world that are relatively backward technologically but also in the best and most modern of our universities. For now, a gene-centered evolutionary materialism may seem to dominate Western culture, but a position of metaphysical dominance tends to be a precarious perch in an ever-changing world.

We do not know now what the world will be like twenty years from now, much less a century, but we do know that the issues now being debated in the universities will play an important role in forming the world of the future. That is why I want to encourage everyone to study the arguments that the scientific atheists of today are making with such confidence. Whether they persuade us or repel us, those arguments will at least encourage us to think about things that universities tended to ignore during the twentieth century and are now absolutely essential to anyone who wants to understand the present, let alone the future. Richard Dawkins and his followers think that a full understanding of Darwinism leads to a realization that our world has no creator and no transcendent purpose. We are confident that a full understanding of the vast difference between what Darwinists claim and what they can demonstrate will reveal that there never was any proof that the Darwinian mechanism of natural selection was capable of performing the fantastic feats of creativity that Darwinists claimed for it.

Darwinism achieved its present dominance not by experimental confirmation but by confident assertion. There is a fatal flaw not just in the outer districts of the Darwinian metropolis but at the very center, with the mechanism that is relied on to perform all the naturalistic miracles. Young people might be encouraged to read widely about Darwinism, from both the perspectives of the standard scientists and the people in the intelligent design movement, and come to their own conclusions about what the "true story" is.

5

THE GOD HYPOTHESIS IN PHYSICS

Phillip E. Johnson

Victor Stenger, an emeritus professor of physics and astronomy at the University of Hawaii, is a relatively unknown but important warrior in the small army of the new wave of scientific atheists. Stenger's book states its thesis with admirable clarity in its title, which is *God: The Failed Hypothesis: How Science Shows That God Does Not Exist.* In the subtitle Stenger makes the bold promise that he will show not just that the case for God's existence is dubious but that an abstract but authoritative entity known as "science" has performed the very difficult feat of proving a negative—that God does not exist.

By *God* (capitalized) Stenger means the personal God worshiped by most Christians, Muslims and religious Jews. What Stenger actually shows is that if God is mischaracterized as a hypothesis in a science devoted to explaining everything in material terms, it (he) is not helpful in furthering that goal. That is a peculiar and unsatisfactory stating of the problem. Considered philosophically, God is not a hypothesis in a science dedicated to physicalism, but a metaphysical platform which is antithetical to physicalism. This theistic metaphysical platform is much more helpful in understanding why our world is governed by rational principles that are accessible to scientific investigation, and why the world contains organisms with the genius of the greatest scientists and of artists like Johann Sebastian Bach and William Shakespeare. Theism was not discovered philosophically merely to plug holes in science despite what Stenger suggests. Natural selection has its proper place in biology, but it does not explain the emergence of extraordinary qualities that would not have furthered the species' reproductive success in the conditions prevailing at the time the human species is supposed to have evolved.

What Stenger means by *science* is harder to make out. Clearly he is not referring to a definition by any authoritative body such as the U.S. National Academy of Science. This Academy actually claims to be neutral on the question of God's existence, although it is emphatically not neutral on the related issue of whether natural (material) causes can explain all events in the history of life. American scientific institutions insist that only naturalistic theories are permitted by their definition of science. Science, these authorities have said, is committed by definition to explaining all natural phenomena by natural causes, and this definition prevents scientists from considering the possibility that an intelligent cause may have been involved in such major innovations as the origin of the first living cell, because they reason that such an intelligent cause would necessarily be supernatural. They say this although they know very well, and sometimes acknowledge when pressed, that they have no adequate naturalistic theory to explain, for example, the origin of the first cell.

Stenger is critical of this exclusion of the supernatural from science by definition, because he thinks that it allows critics of evolutionary naturalism to say that science excludes God from any role in creation on the basis of prejudice rather than evidence. However, he does not attempt to explain how natural causes can create a living cell from nonliving chemicals or evolve a mammal and a bird from a bacterial ancestor. He takes the grand Darwinist story for granted and thus assumes the materialist answers that his philosophy requires.

Although Victor Stenger has sold relatively few books in comparison with the megasellers of Richard Dawkins and Sam Harris, I give his book special attention in this chapter because it is an important intellectual contribution to the new wave of scientific atheism, which should be read by anyone who wishes to understand the movement.

The jacket endorsement by Richard Dawkins explains where Stenger's book fits into the atheist strategy for refuting theistic evolutionists like Francis Collins who do not dispute the Darwinist claim that only purposeless natural forces are responsible for the diversity and complexity of life, but seek to find a role for a creator in setting the cosmic fine-tuning that permitted life to evolve. Dawkins praises Stenger for closing the door to the kind of move from biology to cosmic fine-tuning that Francis Collins attempted in the *Time* magazine debate described here in chapter one. In Dawkins's colorful words,

Darwin chased God out of [Collins's] old haunts in biology and he scurried for safety down the rabbit hole of physics. The laws and constants of the universe, we were told, are too good to be true: a setup, carefully tuned to allow the eventual evolution of life. It needed a good physicist to show us the fallacy, and Victor Stenger lucidly does so. The faithful won't change their minds, of course (that is what faith means), but Victor Stengel drives a pack of energetic ferrets down the last major bolt hole and God is running out of refuges in which to hide.

The best way to describe Stenger's case against the argument for God from cosmology is a question-and-answer format (the answers are Stenger's, not mine):

Question: If the universe is not eternal but had a beginning in the big bang, does this not require that the universe had a cause outside of itself, and thus a creator?

Answer: "The claim that the universe began with the big bang has no basis in current physical and cosmological knowledge. . . . Theoretical models have been published suggesting mechanisms by which our current universe [could have] appeared from a pre-existing one by quantum tunneling or so-called quantum fluctuations." In a popular book, Stephen Hawking proposed a "no boundary" model in which the universe has no beginning or end in space or time.

Extended answer: "Prominent physicists and cosmologists have published, in reputable scientific journals, some other scenarios in which the universe could have come about 'from nothing' naturally. None can be 'proved,' at this time, to represent the exact way the universe appeared, but [the models] serve to illustrate that any argument for the existence of God based on this gap in scientific knowledge fails, since plausible natural mechanisms can be given within the framework of existing knowledge."

Readers may have noticed that although Stenger's ambitious claim is that science has disproved the existence of God, some of his language seems very tentative. He cites only speculative models and "plausible" mechanisms (plausible to whom?), never proof. This is probably because his aim is not really to prove a negative but to argue that when God is proposed as a hypothesis in physics, the hypothesis may not be necessary, because it is possible that scientists may eventually succeed in explaining the phenomenon in question on the basis of natural causes as explanations for events like eclipses or comets. For Stenger, materialist scientists do not need to prove anything to eliminate God from consideration; they can rely on any speculation that promises that a natural cause for any phenomenon may someday be found, even if it does not exist yet.

Stenger does not consider the possibility that God may be something other than a hypothesis in physics in a predominantly materialist inquiry. We, on the other hand, would think of God from a metaphysical platform, from which we can make sense of the world, including the ability of human beings to do physics.

Perhaps the most original aspect of Stenger's argument is that he emphatically rejects the orthodox position of most scientific organizations that science is limited to explaining the natural world and natural causes, and therefore can say nothing about whether God exists or not. Stenger explains that by limiting science to natural causes, these organizations give an argument to those who complain that official science is dogmatically naturalistic.

"However," Stenger continues, "any type of dogmatism is the very antithesis of science." He concludes, "When scientists express objections to claims such as evidence for Intelligent Design in the universe, they are not being dogmatic. They are simply applying the same standards they would for any other extraordinary claim and demanding extraordinary evidence."

The question Stenger ought to have explored at this point is how we are to know what constitutes an extraordinary claim needing extraordinary evidence. Instead, he merely indulges in the assumption that theistic claims are inherently extraordinary and thus disfavored, while naturalistic claims, however fantastic, are inherently part of ordinary science and thus require no proof beyond a judgment of plausibility which can be made by materialists.

If a scientist has published a naturalistic scenario in a professional journal, the requisite showing has been made, no matter how speculative the science. If the scientist is as respected as Stephen Hawking, publication even in a popular book will suffice to refute any suggestion that the evidence of science supports the existence of God. Readers have probably noticed by now that Stenger's approach to the arguments for and against theism is asymmetrical. Theists are expected to produce proof, including proof that no naturalistic solution to the problem of creation is possible. Atheists need only to publish suggestions. Wildly speculative entities like undetectable, alternate universes are perfectly acceptable if they are advanced to refute theism. When the atheists are allowed to enforce one-sided rules like that, the argument is effectively over before it has begun. We might say that Stenger's universe is fine-tuned for atheism.

Question: Where did the laws of physics come from?

Answer: The common belief is that the laws had to come from somewhere outside the universe. But that is not a demonstrable fact. In the often subjective subject of cosmology, we may wonder, what exactly is a "demonstrable fact" and how is it demonstrated? It is true enough that in the often subjective field of cosmology, theorists would have little to do if they relied only on demonstrable facts. There is no reason, writes Stenger, that the laws could not have come from within the universe. He does not explain why a universe that is the product solely of material causes should be lawlike rather than chaotic in its operations. This statement by Stenger in particular could lead to an interesting discussion about the nature of the laws and how they could originate.

Some overall questions could be debated after thinking through the issues raised in this chapter and the preceding ones. How do we avoid believing in things based on authority, especially the authority of science? Where does truth come in? Is it appropriate to evaluate God as a scientific hypothesis?

6

THE OBSTACLE OF OLD BOOKS

John Mark Reynolds

The conversation between theists and non-theists that Phillip Johnson and I hope to see happen faces notable obstacles. The new atheists often misunderstand the books, education and culture of Christians, resulting in miscommunication. It will be my job in the next three chapters to begin breaking down some of these communication barriers.

We are eager for dialogue, but not dialogue that begins with ignorance of what Christians believe or that has no respect for Christian accomplishments.

One of the largest obstacles to dialogue is linguistic. Many of theism's best ideas are found in ancient texts which require training in order to be understood properly. Unfortunately the new atheists do not read these texts well and end up missing the point.

From an academic point of view it is not offensive that new atheists like Richard Dawkins attack the Bible, but it is not helpful that they do not know how to read such books.

They approach these texts with little training in the original languages or how such books ought to be read. This ignorance, however, gives a good student the chance to learn the rules for reading old books.

In his book *The God Delusion*, Richard Dawkins has this to say about the Bible:

> To be fair, much of the Bible is not systematically evil but just plain weird, as you would expect of a chaotically cobbled-together anthology of disjointed documents, composed, revised, translated, distorted and "improved" by hundreds of anonymous authors, editors and copyists, unknown to us and mostly unknown to each other, spanning nine centuries.[1]

It would help if more people with opinions about the Bible knew how to read it.

Secularists reading the Bible are too often like ethnocentric tourists visiting a foreign country. The American tourist who misses great feasts by sticking to McDonalds, because the food of the nation he is visiting is different, is foolish. In the same way, the person who avoids or misunderstands the Bible is missing out.

First, let me agree with Dawkins on one thing: the Bible isn't a simple book; it is at least sixty-six different books collected into a whole. Each discrete book is different; some are very different. The Bible is not a modern novel, it is not a modern history, and it is not a science book. That doesn't mean it does not contain stories, history and scientific truths—just that it is not any of those kinds of books.

Second, the Bible can be the most important book in hu-

---

[1]Richard Dawkins, *The God Delusion* (New York: Houghton Mifflin Harcourt, 2006), p. 237.

man history without being to my taste. Liking a particular work and recognizing greatness in it are two different things. It is easy to despise what we don't like, since it gives us an excuse not to bother with hard work, but the Bible isn't going away.

Third, a billion people base some portion of their lives on it, and their numbers are growing, not shrinking. Islam respects the Bible and that fact creates hundreds of millions more interested religious readers.

Finally, the Bible has motivated much of the great art, philosophy and science of the past. If you don't know the story of the Prodigal Son, then you are going to miss the point of a great many paintings. If you don't read the words of Jesus in the New Testament, then you will miss a great deal of what Abraham Lincoln had to say.

Not surprisingly, the Bible is not as foolish as Dawkins claims. It has endured generations of such critics for very good reasons. The Bible is a stunning work of art and literature when properly understood. Academics, religious and nonreligious, find it worth their entire careers to study a single short book in it.

If God wrote the Bible, then he did so in cooperation with many different human authors. The Bible is not just holy and sacred, it is also human. If it is what it claims to be, then the collection of books called the Bible discloses God to humans as best as can be done. It is a universal message, from God in the ear of humankind, but humans are still limited by their finitude, folly and foibles.

Start reading a book of the Bible the same way you would read any text. Take note of its genre and cultural context. Come with an open mind. As someone who has benefited from ancient literature of all kinds, pagan, Christian and secular, this much is plain to me: Charity to a text broadens thinking and enriches the reader. A reader need not agree with the message, but at least she will know what it is. This will open a meaningful dialogue, instead of one based on misunderstandings.

CHARITY: A BETTER WAY TO READ OLD BOOKS

Reading a text with charity means applying the Golden Rule to a book. We read it hoping for the best and only believing the worst if we must. A good reader attempts to read a book as the author intended.

Why be limited by preconceptions and prejudices when reading? I find it refreshing to attempt, as best I can, to adopt the view of the writer I am reading. Any good reader tries to "get" the book. The best reader first learns what is lovable in any great book and then steps back to see the errors. This can be hard to do with very old books that come from a different time and perspective from our own.

Fortunately, there is a field dedicated to helping people read books, both old and new. This field is called "hermeneutics." Hermeneutics suggests a few key questions to help in reading old books better.

1. Who wrote the book? Who was the first audience? When the author can be known, it may suggest limits to the text or the genre he might have used. It also provides insight into what he may have intended to say.

The first audience for the text is even more important. A modern reader should try, as much as possible, to understand the limits and preconceptions of the original reader. For a biblical book to be written, it must have had all the limita-

72

tions of the words available to the writer and its audience.

If there is no word or concept for a thing, then a biblical book cannot be faulted for failing to use it or teach it. Ancient Hebrew and Greek were what they were. These languages limited what God could say. Just getting the idea of "monotheism" across to Jewish people took centuries of history, argument and experience. Ignoring these limits is at the heart of much ill-informed criticism of what the Bible has to say about human rights.

2. *What am I reading? What kind of book is it?* These questions deal with *genre.*

Genre matters because it helps the reader know what to expect from a book. Poetry has different reading rules than history, and ancient poetry and ancient history have different rules from their modern cousins. Often failure to recognize these rules can lead to foolish errors on the part of a new reader.

Let me give one helpful example. Some genres of ancient literature use numbers in different ways than moderns usually do. When one uses numbers like forty in most modern literature, it usually means the exact amount between thirty-nine and forty-one. This was frequently *not* the case in some genre of ancient literature.

Ancients often used numbers as symbols, though they understood their mathematical use as well. In some forms of ancient literature (such as Genesis and Plato's *Timaeus*) numbers may do both kinds of work, or they may function mostly as symbols. When the first three kings of a united Israel (Saul, David and Solomon) all are said to have reigned forty years, it is likely that something symbolic and not "exact" is being said.

3. How should I read it? What are the rules for reading this particular genre well? Having read up on genre, the good reader now applies the relevant rules to the text in hand. For example, much of the Bible is within the genre of poetry.

A basic form of Hebrew poetry is parallelism. Often an ancient Jewish poet would use a second line to explain or echo the message of a first line. Each line comments on the other. Psalm 2:4 says:

> He who sits in the heavens laughs;
> the Lord holds them in derision.

A good reader would see that one thing was being said in two different ways. The Lord is not worried about human power. God "laughs." This use of a human emotional reaction to describe the Lord is explained when the second line says that "the Lord holds them in derision." The poetic metaphor of God's laughter is a powerful way of stating his scorn for human pride and power. The two lines are best read as one.

4. When was it written? What was the setting? No book is simply timeless or unaffected by the place where it is written. Every work, even one that is divine, is born in a particular place and from a particular people. While many ideas are universal, some are not. Idioms that communicate in one era may not communicate in another. Geographical knowledge that can be taken for granted in one era cannot be taken for granted in another.

A great book, like the Bible, takes a little work to understand the parts that are obscured by changing times, but the effort is worth it for the timeless truths it contains.

5. What would a thoughtful reader, contemporary to the author, have gotten from the book? What did the author intend to say? Authorial intent may not be everything, but it is something. Unless we wish to get nothing more from a book than what we bring to it, the intent of the author is a good way to expand our horizons.

6. *What if the central message is true? Assuming it is true, what are the implications? Is it true?* These are the most exciting questions of all. Imagination is a wonderful tool that allows me to consider the possibility that any religious, philosophical or scientific idea might be true.

This essential need to sympathize with a book in order to "get inside it" is not cultivated in most students. While it is (almost surely) impossible to totally escape our preconceptions, most of us have the experience of "getting into a movie" and forgetting for a moment that it is not real. The movie can drive us to experience love, hate, fear or any other passion. If we can manage it with a motion picture, then why not use our imagination with a book?

New atheists such as Richard Dawkins often forget these six rules for good hermeneutics. And this mistake is often repeated in our universities if the Bible is studied at all. Our universities should be teaching students how to read great literature. I would like to recommend for starters Mortimer J. Adler's *How to Read a Book.* Two excellent works from an evangelical Christian perspective that can help a reader go further are *Playing with Fire* by my university colleague Walt Russell, and *How to Read the Bible for All Its Worth* by Gordon Fee and Douglas Stuart.

CAN OLD BOOKS TEACH US ANYTHING?

Aren't you glad you live *now?* There have never been so many of us with such a high standard of living. It is good to be educated, and many have remarkable access to education. If you were born in the West in the twenty-first century, you have won the lottery of history!

Despite this good news the rates of depression and suicide suggest all is not well. Why aren't we happier?

Part of the reason is the cultural elite believes the only road to knowledge is the scientific. This creates a significant problem for living a good life because science can only describe a narrow slice of what is and it can never tell us what ought to be.

Not only is science blind to the metaphysical, but it cannot tell humanity the importance or value of anything. If a thing exists, then what is it worth? Should there be more of it? Is a human being worth more than a sparrow? Even in the physical realm, science can only tell the physical weight of a thing, not the moral weight a good person should assign it. *Is* can never equal *ought*.

If this is all true, then there exists wisdom that is not scientific. The fact that we live in a golden age of scientific progress does not mean that we live in a golden age. We might be in retrograde motion morally, though advancing scientifically.

Wise old books contain some forgotten lessons. They contain the experiences of men and women in the real world of ethics and the explanations about what their experiences meant. Reading older books like the Bible is a way to become part of this important conversation that since Victorian times has lagged behind the merely technical and vocational.

Critics of the Bible might grant that we should read the book but attack its message. Men like Richard Dawkins and Christopher Hitchens have suggested in recent books that the message of the Bible is monstrous. Dawkins goes as far as to claim that the God of the Old Testament is genocidal and wicked. Is he right? Before answering this question, we will have to make sure that we have not made another literary mistake. If atheists and theists are going to talk, they must make sure they are addressing the real opinions of the other side.

WOULD IT BE ETHICAL FOR GOD TO BE REVOLUTIONARY?

When reading old books, chronological snobbery, as C. S. Lewis called it, is a besetting sin. The chronological snob is to time what the ethnocentric person is to ethnicity. When visiting the past in his imagination, the snob views it as writer and director James Cameron viewed the people of 1912 in the movie *Titanic:* moderns with funny clothes and less stuff.

But Abraham was not an American with sheep and no iPod.

The Lord of sacred Scripture is not a revolutionary, thank God. Rapid change in human culture has rarely been for the best, and God does not make the mistake of the French or Russian revolutionaries. God knows that even a great good must be brought on slowly to avoid doing greater harm.

God must communicate with people in the language and concepts available to them if he is to allow them to mature. Attempting to describe the inner workings of the atom to a tribal people would be useless, since they lack the mental vocabulary to make sense of the message. Of course, God could directly reveal all this to humanity, but this would not allow for natural cultural development or maximum human freedom.

Why is such a development so important? If a culture does not learn for itself what is good, true and beautiful, then it will not be an adult culture. It will depend forever on priest-craft and develop a magical, instead of rational, understanding of reality. We would be lost without divine revelation, but God is intent on giving us the time to truly understand what he is saying. He does not just force it on our imaginations.

Ideas that seem easy to humanity now are the result of thousands of years of human thought in conjunction with the work of God's Spirit. Great genius is often required to understand the big ideas on which later, more incremental progress is based. The very words used to describe and re-fine these ideas must be invented.

As a result, any reader would anticipate that the story of human history in the Bible would be the story of the education of humanity. God would have to tolerate enormous crudities and barbarisms. Jesus Christ, when commenting on Old Testament divorce laws in Matthew 19:8 notes that Moses allowed divorce only because the men of that time had hard hearts.

It is easy for the critic, at the far end of centuries of mostly Christian cultural development, to be critical of the biblical Patriarchs and of the Mosaic law. They forget how stunning and difficult the very idea of a universal law was when God revealed it to Moses. It took hundreds of years for even one people group, the Jews, to grasp the ramifications of a law that applied equally to king and commoner. The morality of "might makes right" was slowly supplanted by "right makes might," but it took thousands of years to do it.

A favorite place of secularists to attack the ethics of the Bible is the narrative of the conquest of Canaan by Joshua. God orders the total (or near total) destruction of the people of the land the Israelites were called to conquer.

The difficulty is applying modern categories of morality, often based on centuries of Jewish and Christian thought, to ancient peoples. They had no language of justice and no concept of "noncombatants." Primitive humans were . . . primitive. They thought in terms of tribe and battled with tribal ferocity.

Humankind, after the rebellion against God, knew only nature red in tooth and claw. Anyone outside the clan or the kin structure was scarcely human. Warfare had no distinction between combatant and noncombatant, and language had no way of thinking about a just war. The god whose people won a war was the "good god." Losing gods were losers.

The Mosaic revelation began to plant ideas that would change all of this thinking. All men and women were created in God's image, not just people in the nation of Israel. All wars in the ancient world were fought brutally, and God commanded that one war be fought that way. His very command that *this* war should be fought as most wars were fought implied that this was an exceptional circumstance, and that other wars should not be fought that way.

In any case, God was dealing with a people who live in a world where they would either be masters or slaves. He had not yet worked with them to create the cultural space that we have for better options. In ancient times the alternative to "total war" was to enslave and intermarry with a small portion of the conquered whom the victors let survive. There was no precedent, no vocabulary, for a just war.

God was faced with an educational problem. He had a group, the Jews, which he was trying to teach the hard lessons of the supremacy of law over passion and of monotheism over polytheism. Old Testament history shows how difficult and arduous this process was. The ancient Jews lived in a time when every surrounding people group would have no qualms about destroying them utterly or making them slaves. Absorbing even the culture of the surrounding nations would simply put off the time when the hard lessons could be properly learned. Extermination was not the rule, but the exception, in any case. The general command in places like Deuteronomy 12 was to avoid the bad practices of the conquered people.

God ordered "total war" against some people groups because it was the best of the bad options available in the time and with the people he had. The total war against the Canaanites minimized their pain by ending it quickly. Enslaving the Canaanites and intermarrying with them also certainly would have infected the nation of Israel with bad ideas that would have made their progress even harder. For most of the conquered people, peace was possible with Israel. There could be total assimilation for most people groups, but not of their bad ideas. God knew Israel could not handle a few groups, and so he had to command total war.

The minute the proper lessons were learned, God taught a more peaceful outlook to the Jewish people. He never ordered them to be an imperial power, none of their great kings were particularly great conquerors, and the lack of emphasis on wars of conquest in their annals is remarkable. God, in his revelation to the Jews, was as interested in what they could learn from losing battles as from winning.

Almost alone in ancient religious literature, the Bible focuses on the failures of the great national rulers more than their victories. We take for granted the ability of the prophet Nathan to confront King David in the Bible (2 Samuel 12), but in most ancient monarchs the prophet would have been dead before making his point. A mark of David's wisdom was that he recognized that God's law came before the will of any human, even a king. This began to root the idea into people's minds that the law was king and the king was not the law.

The long and hard lessons God taught one people would soon be taken to the whole world. Slavery and many other institutions would gradually disappear as the most fundamental principles of the Bible undermined them.

HOW CAN WE KNOW THE BIBLE IS WORTH READING?

Skeptics like Dawkins claim the Bible is not worth our time, but this is just not true. It is easy to propose a simple test to determine if any ancient book is worth our time.

A book is worthy of consideration if it

- has stood the test of time
- describes the general human condition plausibly
- is beautifully written, but also challenging

A book that has endured over a long period of time has good grounds for our consideration. If men and women in the third and the twentieth centuries could find truth in it, then those in the twenty-first should be able to do so as well. This does not mean new books are worthless but that there is likely some basic wisdom in old books that have endured.

When it comes to the most basic ethical assumptions, is the Bible sound? Does it present a plausible general picture of human existence? The Bible very pragmatically notes that this, as a matter of fact, is not the best of all possible worlds.

The Bible is not utopian, but it does try to explain why people wish to live in a utopia.

This book provides a religious basis and motivation for science by postulating a Creator God who is utterly reasonable. It grounds human motivation by arguing that the divine logic is also love. God's logic is moved by God's love.

Finally, the Bible says that all men and woman are created in his image. Before the divine law, all are treated equally. God is just. He wishes us to treat others as we would wish to be treated.

These general ethical considerations have proven both difficult and attractive to people over many centuries. They are stated beautifully and profoundly. When John 3:16 says that God loved the world, it states a deep philosophical truth poetically and succinctly. Whether true or not, it accounts for much we all know to be true about our own existence. We want more than we have and wish to be better than we are. The Bible gives meaning and hope to this experience.

The Bible looks like the kind of ancient book that *might* be true.

ASKING THE RIGHT QUESTIONS ABOUT ANY ANCIENT BOOK

Asking the proper questions about any ancient book can help determine if wisdom can be found in it. The Bible need not be read with any special rules in order to discover its importance.

As a result of reading the Bible with an open mind, generations of people from pagans to skeptics have become convinced it is divine. Both Phillip Johnson and I have devoted our entire lives to following arguments where they lead. Sometimes in our secular academic culture it is considered embarrassing or even impossible for the quest to lead to any answers at all.

We are open-minded enough to be willing to believe the Bible if the Bible turns out to be true. The Bible presents God as unafraid of questions and reasons. He allows his followers, from Jacob to Job, to wrestle with him and ask questions. God could defeat us with the power of his intellect, but he loves us enough to allow us to grow through questions and answers. The Bible is infused with the Holy Spirit, God's Spirit, and needs no other defender, but with the high courtesy of heaven this living book does wait for readers with questions.

7

A WONDERFUL EDUCATION

John Mark Reynolds

The best thing about the new atheists is that they are starting some good conversations. For too long "religion" has been treated as totally private and not subject to scrutiny inside of education. That is too bad, because it infantilizes religion and cuts off a great many interesting conversations.

Conversations about religion can be wonderful and help us all shape a better life for ourselves.

Writing for outlets like the *Washington Post* leads to lots of interesting email. Some critics claim that my job as an educator at a religious institution is hopelessly impractical and a bad deal for my students. Whenever a critic wishes to really let me have it, he or she will point out that I work at Biola University (formerly the Bible Institute of Los Angeles) where the faculty is required to agree with a creedal statement. How can I do philosophy or even real education in such a constricting environment?

Leaving aside the fact that Biola University has not been

a Bible institute for over half a century, the critic is really concerned about the compatibility of faith with reason. Isn't faith the opposite of reason? As one email put it: Christians believe things despite the evidence. If true, that obviously makes living a rational life impossible. For the critic, faith is a set of opinions, and though you can repeat opinions, perhaps in a clever way, you do not need an education to have them.

The critic of religious education argues that it is impossible to be educated without cultivating a spirit of skepticism, but skepticism is antithetical to the religious spirit. Skepticism needs doubt, and doubt is the opposite of faith. Science, philosophy and reason require a Doubting Thomas, while religion wishes to cure Thomas of all his doubts. In the *Los Angeles Times*, biologist P. Z. Myers put it this way:

> It's hard not to take seriously a bizarre collection of antiquated superstitions that are furiously waved in our faces in our schools, on television, in our politics and even on newspaper editorial pages. That we take the intellectually bankrupt beliefs of religion seriously is precisely why we do question it, and will continue to question it, in our boring way: by simply speaking out.[1]

If this series of insults directed at the very idea of religious knowledge and an education with a basis in religion were not enough, there is the idea that education should be practical. The practical person points out that in the modern world most people get education for good jobs or to open up opportunities for better jobs. Religion is not very practical, and at least for most people, it is not very lucrative, and so the

---

[1]P. Z. Myers, "Why Is Charlotte Allen so Mad at Atheists?" *Los Angeles Times*, May 22, 2009.

practical person pushes it to the side. College is too expensive to spend good money thinking about religion.

Students are reduced to mere consumers in a university dominated either by skepticism or an obsession with moneymaking (or both). There is no energy or time left for faith. But this very combination of critics and their ability to live cozily together should make us consider whether there is not a better way. Surely there is more to life than cynicism, debunking and anger. Most of us know from bitter experience that this "something more," happiness, cannot be found in accumulating things. If he who dies with the most toys wins, then it must have been a pretty stupid game to play.

But don't take my word for it or even your own experience. Pick up any catalog from a liberal arts college and read its goals. The college promises so much more than teaching skepticism and moneymaking in return for their expensive tuitions. Is there a better way? There is, and it is the reason that college catalogs still read as if education were about human beings, virtues and is *wonderful*.

WONDER INSTEAD OF DOUBT

The first way to restore beauty and wonder to education is to put skepticism in its place. *Skepticism,* like *gay,* is a word that used to mean one thing and now means something else entirely. It is hard to use it meaningfully at all. Skepticism was a good thing, but now it stands for a toxic attitude that makes genuine happiness difficult.

When Socrates told his young followers to inquire for themselves and not just blindly accept the platitudes of their elders, he was advancing a noble form of skepticism. Socrates thought there was truth and that it was knowable, but that people should look for this truth.[2] The old Athenian recognized that even when we have the right opinions, it is better to examine those opinions and ground them in greater certainty through the use of reason than to stay blissfully ignorant about the basis for our beliefs.

Socrates knew sophists—intellectuals for hire—who attacked the possibility of morality and advocated living for power or pleasure, but he did not give up on either morality or religion. His day was not so different from our own. Socrates looked for a god that was moral and a morality that could make him a better teacher and citizen of Athens. Sophists were skeptical in a caustic way. They mocked Athenian customs when they could not see good reasons for them. Socrates sought to understand what he loved. This was a different kind of skepticism.

His skepticism was one of wonder. He saw goodness, truth and beauty, and wondered what was behind it. He loved the divine; he did not want to debunk it, but his love led him to the natural desire to understand what could be understood. For Socrates, skepticism was wondering about the wonderful.

The skepticism of the sophists tried to take things apart or refute. Socrates might eventually find that a traditional idea was wrong, but sorrowfully. Sophistical skepticism could be initially valuable because it would tear down the pretensions of thoughtless Greek leaders, but it was ultimately parasitic. It could only refute what others asserted. Socratic skepticism would sometimes refute, but in refutation it would try to save what could be saved in the old idea by modifying it. It was constructive and not merely destructive.

---

[2]I am referring to the "Socrates" found in Plato's dialogues. It is difficult to know what the actual Socrates, who wrote no books, believed himself.

In the hands of his greatest student, Plato, education was motivated by love that was produced by wonder at the good, true and beautiful in the cosmos. This love sought to understand the beloved and in doing so often learned painful things, but always sought to save what could be saved of the initial lovely impulse to study. Christianity picked up this idea, so compatible with the life of Jesus Christ, when it came into contact with classical philosophy.[3]

Both dead certainty and endless skepticism tend to crush wonder. Certainty takes the beloved for granted and so never produces motion toward the object of interest. That makes education impossible. Skepticism destroys the love that motivated the desire to learn in the first place. Wonder wants to believe in order to see what is actually true.

Belief is fundamental to education because it provides a hypothesis that can be tested against experience and reason. Experience is gained through life and experiments. Reason, in traditional Christian education, uses open-ended dialogue and examination to test and modify beliefs. Of course, revelation from God provides one kind of experience and data for dialectical discussion in the life of an educated Christian.

Belief combined with wonder allows for faith without foolish certainty. Faith is the best belief that retains what is hoped for within the bounds of best reason and experience. Education is the process of grounding our religious and cultural hopes in long discourse, reason and life experience. The educated religious person is a person of a reasonable and passionate faith. From the compromise between Socratic wonder and Christian theology came the traditional liberal

---

[3]See my *When Athens Met Jerusalem* (Downers Grove, Ill.: InterVarsity Press, 2009).

arts curriculum of the English-speaking world in flagship institutions such as Oxford and Cambridge.

These institutions produced leaders for Christ's Kingdom, called by some *Christendom*. Christendom is the way Christians live inside an imperfect world, before Christ returns and ends time. It is a messy place, but it allows for the best possible life for all people.

AN ELITE EDUCATION FOR THE REST OF US

When most people were farmers, the majority did not need much formal education to gain the virtues necessary to live the good life in their communities. The virtues of a farmer were not complex and (it was believed) did not require the elaborate education of the colleges. As late as the 1920s my grandparents went to school through the eighth grade and could earn respectable middle-class wages and retire in relative comfort. They were educated by the church and by the community to the virtues of their station. Leaders in the culture received more intensive mentoring and training in the liberal arts to prepare them for the ruling class.

Times have changed, thank goodness, and now many people have an opportunity for societal leadership if they have the inclination and ability. The education of the small church or the neighborhood of my grandparents' time is inadequate for the demands of excellence required through the greater responsibilities of leadership.

Sadly, instead of giving more of the rising middle class the traditional, and expensive, education created by Christians in Oxford, Cambridge and other traditional centers of learning, my parents' generation was given job training. There was no confidence that a market economy could expand enough to accommodate the desires of everyone capable of an upper-class education.

College was commoditized and changed to prepare an upper-middle class of compliant middle managers and consumers. Large lecture classes replaced intimate tutorials, and career advisement in factory-sized universities replaced mentoring.

Of course, much good was still done in these schools, as many noble professors worked within the old liberal arts framework, which still existed, to give the best education they could to their students. Large schools also allowed for more efficient research, and all of us have benefited from this change. However, the very success of scientific research tended to overshadow the more pedestrian value of education in the "examined life."

Traditional Christian education has a well-lived life as its goal, but it has death always in mind. For a Christian the good life is a preparation for eternity, but eternity receded in minds trained only to think about their role in the consumer economy. *Time* magazine recently claimed that this generation is consumed with "amortality," the belief that though we will die, it is best to behave as if we never will.

Modern, pragmatic and sophistic education ignores the most important fact known about humans: we are mortal but have eternity in our heart. It is a common contemporary conceit that today's students are much more realistic than the students of the Middle Ages, but the opposite is true. The modern student does not believe in unicorns or death. The medieval student might have believed in unicorns (or not!) but was not stupid enough to doubt that he was mortal. The medieval student was constantly aware of the reality of death and suffering and never ignored it. He was not morbid, but he was not foolish enough to forget how he would end. Modern education creates the magical notion that if death is ignored, it will go away or will not need to be faced. As for eternity, surely if P. Z. Meyers asserts that it does not exist loudly enough, we need not fear it!

This is magical thinking no medieval scholar such as Aquinas would have indulged in for a moment.

Christian education is not to be confused with an apprenticeship program. There is nothing wrong with learning a job skill or the practical skills needed to live in the particular culture in which we find ourselves, but this is not education. Education gives people the capability to do some good with the money that an apprenticeship provides them. It teaches a student virtue. What are these virtues that are missing in so much of our cynical and pragmatic education?

VIRTUE: PREPARING SOULS FOR HAPPINESS

Virtues are the characteristics that allow a human to be excellent at being a human. It might be useful for Joe to be a plumber or a professor, but if Joe is a bad man then his usefulness will be limited, however good he is at fixing pipes or grading exams.

What are the virtues? Christian educators found four in classical philosophy and three from the Bible. The classical virtues are courage, prudence, moderation and justice. The Christian virtues are hope, faith and charity. These are excellences of the soul that come from God, but can be cultivated and strengthened through proper education.

Students are taught to be courageous and moderate through practical guidance and history. Courage is the desire to do what must be done when it is dangerous or particularly difficult to do it. It is taught through physical training and the examples of courageous people from the past. Moderation is the governing principle of the well-lived life. It is taught by a mentor guiding a student in the student's own moral decisions and in looking at great men and women of the past and their decisions.

Prudence and justice are the great virtues of the civilized person. Prudence, or practical wisdom, teaches a person what it is he or she must do. It is taught through experience guided by mentors and by developing a general knowledge of the culture in which a student lives. Justice is treating the equal equally and the unequal unequally. An experience of a wide variety of people and an appreciation of their different qualities through life experience and reading is part of this training. This might provide some common ground in our conversations with nontheists.

In a fallen world classical virtue taken straight can be too strong; however, God reminds us of greater virtues through the revelation of himself in Jesus Christ.

The existence of a good God and an orderly creation is a basis for hope in education. Students do not need to fear any question because the universe is essentially good. They can pursue their studies with hope. Hope grounded in reason and experience becomes faith.

Faith is being willing to act when certainty is impossible. Faith is not certainty but a willingness to follow the argument where it leads. It knows this basic truth: we must commit ourselves, and only then do we see.

All of these virtues are powered by one great virtue: love. A human sees goodness, truth or beauty and loves it. This love drives him or her to know more about the beloved. Fundamentally, Christian education is driven by love to find the object of love and know all that is knowable about the beloved. As a result it is impossible for a Christian, in love with a God he or she believes is good, true and beautiful, to ignore education. Just as any lover will long to know everything there is to know to about the beloved and all his or her works, so the Christian will be passionate to know everything there is to know about God and all his works.

HOW TO TEACH VIRTUE: MENTORING

How are these virtues taught? In classical Christian education they are taught by example. Following the example of Jesus, who walked and taught a group of disciples, the Christian world places a strong emphasis on discipleship. The primary examples come from the mentors or teachers who disciple their students and walk with them toward virtue. The secondary examples are found in the great works of art. These books, movies, paintings and other expressions are, at their best, windows into the image of God found in the great men and women who made them.

Of course, for a Christian this education is centered in coming to know the God-man, Jesus Christ. He is introduced to his student in the pages of the Bible and known by the deepest intellectual and emotional capacities of humankind.

HOW TO TEACH VIRTUE: SEEING FOR ONESELF

Knowing this good person, Jesus, helps us become like him.

The central story that explains this education of the soul is found in the biblical book written by Luke. In chapter twenty-four of his account of the ministry of Jesus, Luke tells of two disappointed disciples who were walking home after the crucifixion of Jesus. Jesus comes to them, but hides his identity from them. He asks them questions about their feelings and allows them to express their great sorrow and bewilderment. Jesus then teaches them from the Scriptures how his suffering and death were predicted and was the culmination of history to that point.

When I was a child, I did not understand why Jesus hid his identity from these disciples. Why didn't he just heal their pain by appearing to them? One day sitting in church, I realized an answer to this question: if Jesus had ministered to their felt needs by appearing to them in glory, he would have ended all discussion. He could have healed the surface wounds of his disciples, an important thing to do, but his glory would have left the disciples unable to do anything but marvel, and Jesus wanted them to think and assent to his message with all their heart, soul and *mind.*

His disciples had bad ideas, and Jesus wanted adult followers, not mindless robotic drones. He hid his overwhelming glory from them so they could *learn.* He taught by questions and discussion, and then revealed himself finally to them in the breaking of the bread.

Jesus Christ is a perfect example for a teacher. He dealt with the deep needs of his students and not just the problems he knew they had. Jesus asked questions and allowed his students to give bad answers. He used a great text that they had read and discussed its meaning with them. Jesus raised his students to a higher level and did not just crush them with his superior understanding and experience.

Luke does not give the details of Jesus' teaching, and so I wondered about this missing part of the story. Why set it up so carefully and then leave out most of what Jesus said? It struck me forcefully one day that Christ wanted to walk with me, allow me to ask questions and also appear to me at the end of this discipleship process in the sacraments of the church. Luke did not short circuit the process for me, either, by telling me the Lord's teaching.

Jesus is the model educator, and Luke imitated his technique in writing his Gospel.

Of course, there were other great teachers who contributed to the Western view of education, including the great philosophers of the ancient world. Their truth was heard and appropriated when discovered by the church. Christianity contributed important ideas to the development of education and will continue to do so, but it does not, in itself, contain *all* truth. Christian education has benefited from contributions by Islamic, Jewish, pagan and secular thinkers over the centuries. While every generation of Christians has contained purists who were not open to ideas from outside sources, they have rarely dominated the mainstream of Christian education. Examining every idea and appropriating that which was helpful is a long-standing Christian tradition.

EDUCATION, CHRISTIANITY AND OTHER FAITHS

I have spent the last fifteen years putting some of these ideas into practice at the Torrey Honors Institute at Biola University. With a dozen highly trained professors, we have educated hundreds of students, and the results have been amazing. We have sent graduates—from opera singers to missionaries—into the entire world. Because we teach ideas that both favor and oppose Christianity, a few have chosen to leave the faith. Most have remained faithful witnesses to the compatibility of a traditional Christian message with an examined life.

The best thing about Torrey has been the creation of an authentic community of learners. Teachers and students are learning together. While I started the program, I am no longer necessary to it, but am able to enjoy the learning that goes on in Torrey every day. It is not some educational paradise, for we often fail to live up to the high standards of the Master, but it is living proof that the Socratic method has nothing to fear from the lordship of Christ.

Jesus is Lord of all creation and of every human, and so we have found joy in learning even from those who do not share our faith. Since all humans are created in God's image, Christians certainly do not have a lock on doing education well. Christianity may have invented the university and put together the principles for best education in the West, but knowing what to do is not, sadly, the same thing as doing it. Torrey has experienced in a small way the hard-earned wisdom of listening to the wise man or woman outside the faith.

I know a man who is almost eighty, but has spent his entire life pursuing wonder, not skepticism. He has lived a good life because he is neither credulous nor cynical. He is full of wonder. Is he a Christian? I do not know, but he lives as a Christian should in his educational philosophy.

Torrey owes him a great debt.

It is therefore more than possible to be a great educator without being a Christian. But can a non-Christian culture sustain an educational system created from the fusion of Christianity and Greco-Roman thought? Perhaps, but it has proven very difficult for even Christians to sustain it, and the present situation does not look hopeful. Without a revival of traditional Christianity, the open-ended quest may deteriorate into mere cynicism, trendiness or practicality with nothing human left at all.

If wonder and a thirst for goodness, truth and beauty are enough to sustain an education, then a Christian has the necessary characteristics to be educated. Of course, this is not a process that a Christian believes will end before death, for then his or her education in even deeper things will just be beginning. Heaven will be utterly wonderful.

8

CHRISTIANITY AND BEAUTY

John Mark Reynolds

When my father was a boy most people who said something was "Christian" meant it was decent or good. However insensitive this was to religious minorities in the United States, the term *Christian* had less religious and more moral connotations, and they were mostly positive. Things have changed so much that my teenage children now have the general rule that if a Christian appears in a contemporary book or film, the character will almost surely be villain. If not, then it is an infallible sign that a Christian produced it!

Traditional Christians are stereotyped as the "bad guys" so often that a few critics have gone even further. Perhaps the most extreme is the professional pundit Christopher Hitchens. He claims that religion is *always* harmful and that it does no good for culture. Religious people may do good things, but it is despite their religion, not because of it. "Anything Christians do, atheists can do better" is a decent summary of his taunts.

The experience of terrorism and Islam combined with the memory of persecution by Christian authorities has made it easy for people like Hitchens to attack religion. Hitchens also ends *God Is Not Great* with an appeal for even *more* sexual liberation in Western nations. Apparently the problem is that we are still too hung up about sex. However laughably implausible this sounds to anyone who deals with college students, Hitchens at least has taken up a popular cause. It is always easier to shout "Party on!" than to point out that the bills for the party may be coming due.

Mere lack of faith is not enough for Hitchens. He loathes, hates and despises religion, and has made a decent living doing it. He says:

> I am not even an atheist so much as I am an antitheist; I not only maintain that all religions are versions of the same untruth, but I hold that the influence of churches, and the effect of religious belief is positively harmful. Reviewing the false claims of religion, I do not wish, as some sentimental materialists affect to wish, that they were true. I do not envy believers their faith. I am relieved to think that the whole story is a sinister fairy tale; life would be miserable if what the faithful affirmed was actually the case.[1]

How plausible is Hitchens's attack on religion? Atheism and agnosticism have generally been tiny movements in Western history. As a result, they have not done much in relative terms, good or bad, because they have had so few followers. Sometimes they have tried to inflate their numbers by claiming deists like Thomas Jefferson or Thomas

---

[1]Christopher Hitchens, *Letters to a Young Contrarian* (Cambridge, Mass.: Basic Books, 2001), p. 55.

Paine, but deism, the belief in a Creator not personally involved in his creation, is religious. Despite their relative unimportance in Western history, atheists and agnostics now claim to be the one true nonfaith.

Hitchens claims religion holds back civilization, but there are no great world civilizations not born and maintained in religion. It would be more plausible, though a bit uncharitable, to suggest that secularism has been parasitical on theism's successes and failures.

WHAT IT MEANS AND WHY IT MATTERS

Why does all of this matter? Surely Hitchens is such an amusing blowhard that nobody will take him seriously! Sadly, Christopher Hitchens is telling many people what they want to hear. Organized religion has had a series of well-publicized failures and scandals in this century. Many people have experienced those failures or read about them. Islamic terrorists are allowing atheists to escape their Cold War stigma as a few of our allies against godless communism turn out to be pretty bad themselves.

Religious groups are community-centered in an individualistic age. People want to do their own thing without being told what to do by someone else. This is particularly true when it comes to self-indulgence. Prudence and moderation are hard to practice and impossible to preach in a land where the profit motive drives endless commercials and programs promote, if not cause, imprudence and immoderation. It is uncertain if such individualism is an adequate basis for a community, but most Americans are cocooning too much to notice.

There are bad things done in the name of any given religion. The hope is that by listing religious faults and pounding them into young minds, Hitchens will shame many Westerners out of any association with religion at all.

AN OPPORTUNITY FOR BETTER UNDERSTANDING: A NEW PERSPECTIVE ON THE STORY

Secularists have a good story to tell. Like all myths theirs is powerful and unites many disparate facts, making sense of them. In this story, Western humanity gradually outgrows a "magical view" of reality. People move from polytheism to monotheism under the pressure of the growth of philosophy and (eventually) science. Evangelistic secularists frequently say that the monotheists are just like atheists, except they cling to a belief in one last god!

The secular myth continues with a page from drawn from the eighteenth-century historian Edward Gibbon: Christianity destroyed classical civilization and brought on a Dark Age.[2] Civilization escaped the Dark Ages only with the rise of the Renaissance man and science. Secular thinking helped shake off the shackles of religion and created the modern world. Today only the vestiges of organized religion prevent humankind from achieving its full potential. Helping "sell" this story is the promise that secularism finally will allow total personal freedom, especially in the area of sexuality. This is a point that Hitchens makes explicit at the end of his jeremiad *God Is Not Great*.

Christian apologists often miss the power of this myth when debating evangelistic secularists like Hitchens. In 2009, my oldest children watched William Lane Craig de-

---

[2]The extent of Gibbon's actual distaste for organized religion is debatable. That evangelistic secularists repeat his framework of Western history uncritically is not.

bate Christopher Hitchens. If the argument was about the existence of God or had been scored on who made the best use of evidence and reason, Craig destroyed Hitchens. But, as my children pointed out, Hitchens told the better, more coherent story. He did not have much evidence for this tale and could not defend it in detail, but he told it well and it was attractive due to its extreme simplicity.

The good news for Christian theists is that Hitchens's story is simple to the point of being simplistic, and they have a better story to tell. The basic story is this: the combination of Greek philosophy and Christianity produced Christendom, which has produced most of the great goods of our world. Christendom provides a home for both reason and meaning. It balances law and liberty. It makes love the central motive for human action and a reasonable God the end of that love. While Christians often fail, the basic ideas of Christendom keep pulling humanity back from the brink of utter tyranny or ruinous social chaos. Christian failures create secularists, who often serve as useful in-house critics of Christian inconsistencies. Moderate secularists often make useful and important subsidiary contributions to institutions created by Christians, such as hospitals and universities. At their worst, evangelistic secularists are destructive cynics parasitically living within Christian-built structures and undermining their philosophical and theological basis for existence.

In ancient times Western humans veered between worshiping too much (polytheism) and too little (atheism). Both problems fed on each other and prevented the full development of science and philosophy. Polytheism made the universe too chaotic to be studied with reason, and atheism constantly threatened to turn into cynicism or undermine meaning. These cultural problems inevitably led to tyranny of either the masses or an educated elite.

A few philosophers, such as Plato and Aristotle, proposed monotheism, which was very different from the polytheism of the idol worshipers. The "one God" of the philosophers was not simply a bigger Zeus or Zeus without rivals, he was a different type of being altogether. From the point of view of monotheism, polytheists don't worship a god at all. Monotheism did not prune the "god garden"; it developed a wholly new species of being. Unfortunately, neither Plato nor Aristotle managed to find a political system that could balance the rights of the individual with the creation of a stable social order necessary for civilization.

Judaism was the most successful monotheistic religion in the ancient world, and it found deep compatibility with monotheistic ancient philosophy. Jewish thought had successfully placed the rule of law over the power of governments. This gave the religion an inherent tendency to balance individual liberty with central control. The prophet could rebuke the king in Judaism, but there was no utopian belief in the inherent goodness of the individual either. Jesus Christ and his apostles came to found a church, not an earthly empire. The kingdom of heaven is not ultimately of this world and his children are fundamentally are not at home this side of his coming. There remains for Christians, however, the time between the first coming of Jesus and his second coming.

During this time, Christians live and work out their beliefs with God's help as best they can. They can learn a great deal from non-Christians about how to live in the here and now, because all people possess God's image.

The church was born in a Greek and Roman world and learned some good lessons from both. The result was a sometimes messy amalgamation that has had real social benefits for both non-Christians and Christians.

Sadly, Christians faced a secular tyranny backed by popular paganism that attempted to stamp them out. In the Eastern Roman Empire, government persecution eventually collapsed and Christendom gave the empire another thousand years of life. Though Eastern Christians often misunderstood their own best principles and made grave errors applying them, they preserved and studied the best of Greek and Roman philosophy, contributed their own ideas and created a remarkable and beautiful culture. They experienced no real "dark age" and continued to make remarkable cultural progress and innovation in government, art, religion and philosophy right to the end of their rule. Their cultural evolution was impeded by a constant need to defend themselves against external foes, often misbehaving Christians! Eventually the Eastern Empire would be conquered by Turkish invaders (1453) but not before passing the fruits of their labor to Western Christians. The Renaissance was deeply indebted to their religiously motivated labor.

The West faced a more difficult situation due to external conquest. Society collapsed under pressure from pagan barbarians or lightly converted Germanic tribes. The Western Roman Empire went through several hundred years of troubles, and the Christian church preserved what was saved of the previous civilizations. Fairly rapidly all over Western Europe, religions institutions, such as monasteries, began to regain cultural momentum. They created great art and music, and began to develop the philosophical ideas that would produce science, the modern university and more liberal forms of government.

This progress was not, of course, linear. Christians made mistakes, had false starts and would fall short of their highest ideals. However, when moderate Islamic scholars introduced new concepts into the thirteenth-century Christian world, it found a lively and mostly receptive culture. Eastern Christian thinkers who found congenial students in places such as Northern Italy aided this development.

Brilliant thinkers like Thomas Aquinas and great writers such as Dante created interesting and important philosophical and mythological systems that spurred cultural progress. Great strides were made in the natural sciences, the arts, government and philosophy. The Black Death slowed this momentum, but the fall of the Eastern Empire brought new scholars and manuscripts to Europe. The bedrock ideas for international law, the university system, more democratic forms of government, and science were developed.

Of course, this growth was impeded by the mistakes and errors of Christians all along the way. There is an endless catalog of folly and sin committed by Christians, because for this seminal period Christians were almost the only meaningful system of thought. Blame Christians for their faults surely, but credit Christendom for its greatness. In fact, the internal divisions of Christianity in the West eventually allowed more secular philosophies to begin to hijack the development of culture. Fundamentally, however, it was the overwhelmingly Christian populace, politicians and societies that continued to work out the practical implications of the Christian message.

Against this practical truth, Hitchens can only weakly claim that secularists could have invented science, the university system and modern forms of government. But this is a nonfalsifiable claim, because Western Christians, with the help of other theists such as Jews and Muslims, already did those great deeds. It is easy to claim to be able to do a thing after it has been done, but hundreds of years of Greek and Roman thought prior to the coming of Christianity had not managed to do it. As Europe and the rest of the West secularize, even Hitchens worries that his fellow evangelistic secularists may not have the will to defend or maintain the civilization they inherited.

Of course, evangelistic secularists also face the horrible tragedy of the twentieth century, where millions were killed in the name of atheism. Faced with this record, Hitchens often blames Christians for their own martyrdoms. In Russia, for example, he claims that Orthodox Christianity created the top-down and subservient culture that allowed the atheist Stalin to kill. Hitchens chooses to ignore a century of evangelistic secular writing, which advocated bloodshed and revolution both inside and outside of Russia.

His history of Russia is remarkably similar to communist propaganda history that blamed all failures on "old Russia" and took all credit for the Russian success. He ignores the fact that a remarkably irreligious Peter the Great made the Orthodox Church a mere department of the state and limited its freedom of action. He ignores the fact that even so, the Orthodox Church had succeeded in radically reducing the use of the death penalty and increased the rights of prisoners, and that Orthodox communities were creating powerful local and fairly democratic institutions. Orthodox Russia rapidly was evolving into a constitutional monarchy. Of course, the last Russian tsar, himself a pious man, made the horrific mistake of trying to retard this natural progress, but Orthodox Christians were numerous in opposing his errors and working within the system to correct them. They were largely succeeding in laying the framework for a greater and more liberal Russia within the framework of an Orthodox faith. Literacy was growing, cultural achievements in the arts have never been matched in Russian history, and economic inequalities, while still horrible, were being addressed in the late tsarist period.

Secular takeover ended all hope of progress. Stalin and later secularists reduced the rights of prisoners and made their treatment more barbaric. Secularists reduced regional social progress and democratic structures. They killed reactionary Orthodox priests and politicians, but they also killed liberal Orthodox priests and politicians. They put in place a Russian constitution more backward than the one gained in 1905. Over a century of gradual societal evolution was ended. To pretend that secularists simply built on "religious tyranny" is a blood libel.

Finally, even if Hitchens could manage to place the blame for butchery in Russia on the Christians being butchered, it is difficult to claim that the secular government in Asia is doing the same. In China, a Protestant Christian Sun Yat-sen tried to create a republic. The more faithfully secularized Chinese, who took their atheism straight, developed Mao, who destroyed any hope for liberty and killed millions. Was religion to blame for Mao? If so, then how was it? Christianity in China produced some noble leaders and some corrupt ones, but secularism produced monsters. It would be difficult to blame historic Christianity for atheism's failures in China.

The story of secularism is positive only when it has theism to criticize. It has shown no long-term capacity to govern and sustain a culture. Even Western Europe could not be described as truly secular until well after the Second World War. English religiosity was much like that of the United States well through the 1950s. Is there sufficient evidence of cultural vibrancy or confidence, or an ability to defend its values in secular Western Europe for Hitchens to be so confident that the United States should follow the Western European lead?

Secularism is destructive for three reasons. First, it cuts off the elite from the common people. A Christian professor believes he or she should not steal for the same reason a Christian farmer believes that stealing is wrong. The professor may have more elaborate justifications for his or her beliefs, but they are just an extension of the farmer's. There is no such close connection between the moral beliefs of the secular professor and the secular farmer, unless the belief that there are no binding ethical principles beyond preference counts. The rising tensions between populism and elitism in Western culture will find no solutions in Hitchens's secularism. The problems are difficult enough for Christians who have a common moral base!

Second, secularism invents its own meaning for life. This may work for a few who develop Stoic virtues, but for most people it tends toward self-indulgence and hedonism. Why should a person fight and die to defend grandchildren he or she will never see? There may be atheists in foxholes, but historically there are precious few of them. Hitchens loves European culture and wants to see it defended, but on what basis will he convince others to die for it?

Even if we imagine that external threats somehow disap-pear, or that the very religious United States will continue to pay most of the bill for Europe's defense by maintaining a large deterrent and strong alliances, what will motivate social sacrifice internally? Why shouldn't politicians steal if they think they can get away with it? Of course graft and corrup-tions are not solved by religion, but every study shows that if a person thinks God is watching, he or she is less likely to cheat and steal. Secularism makes a bad problem worse by removing an important restraint to corruption. I would wish Hitchens good luck maintaining the rule of law in a secular-ized Europe, but Europe will not remain secular.

Finally, secularism has trouble self-correcting once it does a bad thing, because there is no universally admired secular standard a secularist can appeal to. When the Inquisition did barbaric things, Christians could and did criticize it within the faith. It ended because it was inconsistent with basic Christian principles, and populations that were overwhelm-ingly Christian would not tolerate it. What are the common principles of global secularism? How are they grounded? Who will be their prophets to rebuke their kings and on what basis?

Secularism has shown no positive agenda. Let us assume for a moment that the secularists were to get all that they want in the United States. Abortion and same-sex marriage would cease to be issues. Christianity would vanish from the public square. Then what? Science cannot give us *ought,* it can only describe what *is.* What will secularists propose for a positive program once the theist boogeyman is gone? What really unites them other than opposition to religion?

Humankind has shown no ability to accept evangelistic secularism in large numbers. Most people will use it to tear down moral restraints or systems they don't like, but then, in the short term, embrace some sort of moral therapeutic deism in its place. In some places "deism" will be replaced by real magic or paganism.

What will they select if times get very bad, as times often do? What will limit their irrationality if the great monotheistic faiths, which at their heart believe in reason, are no longer around? It is true that the great faiths (Judaism, Christianity and Islam) have not always been faithful to their followers, but on what positive basis will secularists judge their own excesses?

Secularists did not build on centuries of stagnation; they helped destroy a great deal of cultural progress Orthodox Russia had made over the centuries. They slowed down rates of positive change, but then took credit when the positive changes took place despite them. Orthodox Russia had a long tradition of scientific advancement and cultural excellence, which even radical secularists could not eradicate. In fact, it was nationalism and pride in those achievements that often saved Russia from the worst excesses of secularism!

If human beings are naturally religious, it appears that Hitchens and Dawkins are most likely to stamp out religions that are the best for society. If they succeed in shaming Westerners out of fairly peaceful religions that created the modern world, what will replace those faiths? Atheism and agnosticism have not shown any remarkable abilities to quell superstition in Western Europe. The cabbie who gives up on the Church of England because he does not like its moral rules instead reads his horoscope daily.

As I write this, I am preparing to leave for Florence, a city so full of beauty that I have to take it in slowly to keep from being overwhelmed by it. This great culture was created by an amalgamation of Eastern Christianity, the best of Greek philosophy (especially religious Platonism) and Roman Christianity. It led to a flowering of art, culture, science and political reform in one small city that surpasses anything done in Athens. Not all the players in Florence were Christians, some were even secular, but from Dante to the Florentine Academy it was the fusion of Christian and religious Greek thought that changed the world. Sometimes persecuted by other Christians and at other times aided by them, since almost all power was in Christian hands, these Christians and theists are a splendid model of the power of rational religion to renew itself and bring positive change.

Evangelistic secularism and evangelistic theism can both produce tyrants and ugliness. Popes persecuted the Florentine Academy, but religion created it. There is no evidence that over time secularism can produce a Michelangelo or create a culture that can widely appreciate him. Like many overzealous people evangelistic secularists struggle with beauty blindness. Insofar as they are consistent secularists, they can listen to Mozart or watch Shakespeare, but cannot really understand their depths. Fortunately, most secularists are not entirely consistent!

Christians must not persecute evangelistic secularists. Our errors have blinded them to beauty and caused them to turn away from civilization. Yet the good fruit of Christendom, including the university and science, still attract the better part of evangelistic secularists, who are still souls created in the image of God. We can trust that God, Father of our achievements and who suffers with us in our errors, will continue to draw them back to himself. That at least is a traditional Christian perspective on old books, education and culture. It is based on wonder and is always hopeful. But of course one thing that any Christian wonders is if he is correct. We don't want to be Christians if Christianity is false.

One thing Christianity encourages us to do is to wonder about our own beliefs! We are people of faith and not certainty, even in our own faith. Augustine encouraged us to have faith in search of understanding, not in search of more faith. Both of us have our doubts and we try to pursue those doubts honestly, reasonably and with integrity.

We have presented our perspective and hope that the new atheists can grow and interact with real Christianity to the benefit of both. The culture can only benefit if all of us keep talking. We, as Christians, look forward to the conversation.

EPILOGUE

Phillip E. Johnson

In April 2009, the brilliant historian and journalist A. N. Wilson published an article explaining why, after twenty years of atheism, he has become a Christian believer once again. In his leap to atheism twenty years earlier, he had a "Damascus road experience," while the return to faith has been slow and doubtful at every step. In retrospect, he thinks he should have distrusted the symptoms that accompanied his conversion experience to atheism, because something was happening which was out of character—the inner glow of complete certainty, the heady experience of being at one with a great tide of fellow believers.

Much later, when the glow of conversion and comradeship had worn off, Wilson realized that religion is not matter of argument alone. It involves the whole person. He was drawn again and again to the disconcerting recognition that many of the people he had most admired and loved, either in life or in books, had been believers. He greatly admired the skeptical arguments of the Scottish philosopher David Hume, but on reflection he thought that Hume did not confront the complexities of human existence as deeply as his contemporary Samuel Johnson, nor was he as interesting. He also decided that purely materialist explanations for the mystery of human existence simply will not do, on an intellectual level. The materialists sounded convincing when they were attacking Christianity, but their own creed of materialism was not convincing at all to him. Doubts piled upon doubts, and eventually he found that his skeptical nature led him out of atheism and back to the Christian faith that he had left for atheism.

The lesson I draw from Wilson's experience is that every position about the nature of life and its origin has difficulties. Therefore, the question is not whether we can find a position that has no difficulties, but rather, which set of difficulties we prefer to embrace. We also need to be a little skeptical about the ability of our own minds to find truth in a jungle of competing claims. Wilson thought he had found truth at the time of his conversion to atheism, but in retrospect it seemed more as if he was joining a fashionable movement. It is hard for us to know when we are being perfectly rational, or when we are simply following the dictates of fashion. This does not mean that we should stay away from difficult philosophical or scientific reasoning, but that we should be careful not to give it too much importance in our lives. Arguments play an important role in the life of the mind, but in the final analysis, humans do not live by argument alone but by the whole picture of life, as Wilson later came to realize.

Index